Obedience is Freedom

Obedience is Freedom

Jacob Phillips

polity

First published in 2022 by Polity Press

Polity Press
65 Bridge Street
Cambridge CB2 1UR, UK

Polity Press
101 Station Landing
Suite 300
Medford, MA 02155, USA

ISBN-13: 978-1-5095-4933-7 (hardback)
ISBN-13: 978-1-5095-4934-4 (paperback)

A catalogue record for this book is available from the British Library.

Library of Congress Control Number: 2021949835

Typeset in 9.5 on 14 pt Fournier
by Cheshire Typesetting Ltd, Cuddington, Cheshire
Printed and Bound in the UK by TJ Books Limited

The publisher has used its best endeavours to ensure that the URLs for external websites referred to in this book are correct and active at the time of going to press. However, the publisher has no responsibility for the websites and can make no guarantee that a site will remain live or that the content is or will remain appropriate.

For further information on Polity, visit our website:
politybooks.com

Contents

Introduction

Readers picking up a book entitled *Obedience is Freedom*, with chapters entitled 'Allegiance', 'Loyalty' or 'Obligation' and so on, may be expecting an academic treatise. Perhaps they will expect this introduction to start by listing some examples of how obedience is today considered irredeemably toxic. Then, a discussion of freedom, suggesting today's preference for interpreting this as individual self-fulfilment often leaves people frustrated, isolated and at times even enslaved. The ground would then be prepared to state the thesis of this book: a rediscovery of obedience (and subcategories like allegiance, loyalty and obligation) promises a more enduring and genuine freedom than that offered by today's self-fulfilment paradigm. Indeed, many great thinkers have long since argued that an avoidance of restraint serves only to intensify the degree to which we are restrained, and that genuine and enduring freedom is to be found through obediently entering into the ways personal choice is ever limited by the networks of responsibility in which we live.

Having outlined the basic position in the Introduction, such readers might expect the chapters to outline, in prosaic terms, exactly how the themes under discussion contribute to that more authentic freedom lacking in today's world. These would then begin with comments on the etymology of the chapter heading. These terms often combine elements of restraint or obedience with expressions of spontaneity or freedom. The word obligation, for example, derives from the past-participle stem of the verb *obligare*, meaning 'to bind', and yet also from the noun *obligatio*, which is connected with expressing gratitude; hence the old English phrase 'much obliged'. From findings such as these, some discussion of ancient texts would be expected, particularly those of Greek and Roman philosophy. Then a critical discussion with more contemporary voices could follow, working towards the overarching conclusion that obedience is not only connected with freedom in ways we seem to have forgotten, but that these two are so mutually dependent they are indistinct: hence, obedience is freedom.

A reader expecting a book of this nature, however, will not find it in this volume. This is not a systematic or polemical text that seeks only to argue in explicit and straightforward terms. Rather, the book includes concrete histories describing specific events from the last three or four decades. It also engages not only with writers on obedience and freedom, but with literary interlocuters like Charles Dickens and Karl Ove Knausgaard, neither of whom would usually be expected to be found in a book of this nature. While there is philosophical discussion, there are biographical reminiscences too and much material that is taken from my own life, particularly in drawing on cultural phenomena that others of a similar age and background might recognize.

Discerning readers who want to understand the sources for the notion of freedom that underpins this book are recommended to read some St Augustine and Dietrich Bonhoeffer (which is not to say I pretend either thinker would endorse this book). Those wanting to understand more recent discussions would be advised to read Patrick Deneen's *Why Liberalism Failed* and maybe *The Cunning of Freedom* by Ryszard Legutko. Readers of this book need to know why *Obedience is Freedom* has been written in an offbeat way.

This stems firstly from the intellectual fecundity of more offbeat realms of discourse in the UK and USA, particularly, since around 2016. As a young academic, I took great interest in witnessing freer, more engaging and often more genuinely insightful work emerge in obscure online publications than in peer-reviewed journals and the volumes of academic publishing houses. Rather than argue the now well-worn trope of 'this thing you think is left-wing is actually conservative' and vice versa, it seemed more effective to enter into such things with elements of narrative. Concrete stories and their atmospheres disclose things that contemporary presuppositions struggle to relate. A great many conceptual binaries beside obedience/freedom have been broken in recent years, but these binaries can be glimpsed in a restored state by observing how they interrelate in recent history.

If there is a method on display here, it is synaesthetic – an attempt to bring together things we cannot imagine being the same, like seeing smells or hearing the sensation of touch. These types of interrelations are often only lightly buried in the recent history of Western cultures, just under the surface, where obedience and freedom can still be seen as two sides to the same coin, each requiring the other.

Secondly, while it has become increasingly apparent that much interesting writing is happening 'outside' the authorized platforms and credential system, the content of this writing is often similarly 'outside' dominant ideological paradigms. These paradigms are most commonly associated with identity politics, although its roots go back much further, as I argue later on. A discourse that takes place 'outside' the dominant worldview reminded me of a time when alternative manners of living were being explored by those then 'outside' mainstream society, particularly in the 1990s. For me, the two forms of 'outsideness' can inform each other, just as the themes and concepts of this book were once subtly linked together. There is much to be learned, albeit often negatively, about how things like 'allegiance', 'obligation' or 'respect' were bound up with the alternative worldviews of peaceniks, squatters, travellers or road protestors. That is, with people thought to be archetypal seekers of freedom.

Thirdly, I would say that the 'conservatism' on display in the pages of this book is of a broadly postmodern character. This does not mean surrendering to moral or cultural relativism, by any means, but involves a focus on how writers are implicated in their subject matter and vice versa. It means writing from the point of contact between self and world, because the juncture of subjectivity and objectivity discloses things that an exclusively subjective or objective approach does not. This sort of postmodernism is, paradoxically, exactly what those associated with 'postmodern ideology' today have entirely neglected, while claiming to celebrate it in abundance. Identity characteristics are frequently foregrounded in every discussion, but not fostering freedom of exploration and expression so much as closing everything down to a mere monologue. Those who would most explicitly celebrate the interrelation of subject and object are today those most likely to break the binary between the two, so only one remains, under the rubric of 'lived experience' (see Chapter 5). In any case, I lived through much of what is written in this book. It amused me no end when the editors of an online journal tagged an essay I'd written in this style as 'fiction'. No word of this book is fiction.

The reasons just listed give some indication as to why I chose not to write this book using standard means of argumentation like those described at the outset. But before leading people into the countryside of West Berkshire in the early 1980s, the record shops of mid 1990s Hackney, or the exodus to Cornwall to watch the solar eclipse in 1999 – it is only fair that I at least offer some preliminary orientation to show how the chapters work towards the claim that obedience is freedom.

Chapter 1, 'Allegiance', highlights the obedience involved in child-bearing and child-rearing, entailed by the visceral attachment of mother and child. Changing attitudes to natality based on wanting a greater freedom, I contend, are symptomatic of one of the great challenges of our age, in which mutual allegiance one for another in a shared culture is perpetually at risk of fracturing and fragmentation, of warring cultures within one society. A culture that celebrates the commonality of mother and child is one set free to celebrate its own commonality on a societal scale. A culture that is hostile to the most visceral commonality is one that threatens to lose all sense of common ground whatsoever.

Chapter 2, 'Loyalty', focuses on a surreptitious slip in the understanding of the obedience associated with this term, whereby it is made secondary to personal choice: being loyal to those with whom you agree or towards whom it is advantageous to evince loyalty. The chapter enters into critical discussion with Jonathan Haidt, David Goodhart, Christopher Lasch and Peter Sloterdijk, who have each tried in different ways to interrelate the legitimacy of loyalty to one's society or culture within an age of rapidly changing values and views among citizens. The chapter concludes that loyalty is the fruit of freedom, not its opposite; that cherishing the ways people share belonging enables them to let that belonging take precedence over optionality and preference without entailing anything abusive or toxic.

Chapter 3, 'Deference', is based on the position that many of the ills of today's world are rooted in the dissociation of people from the networks of responsibility by which we live. Self-fulfilment, as social mobility, is presented as fostering a literal self-centredness, whereby one's position in society is made the measure of personal worth, one's centre. By contrast, and exemplified in the novels of Charles Dickens, I argue that moral and economic worth or dignity must never be confused, that one's moral value, or centre, is bound up with the good of the whole to which one contributes. I also argue that separating moral and economic value can liberate people from the various narratives of affliction that pervade our culture, because those narratives serve to cover up the various issues with self-esteem and mental illness that attend aggressive meritocracy. The ability to defer is indicative of a society where moral and economic worth are disambiguated – for deferring to others is acutely painful if their perspective is deemed representative of some sort of greater dignity than one's own. Deference just means accepting another's viewpoint as better placed than one's own.

Chapter 4 is entitled 'Honour' and turns to love, sex and desire in the internet age. The point here is that obediently accepting another's standing as an 'end in itself' and never a means to one's own ends, in a loving relationship, means honouring that person as someone who is not ensnared in one's own schemes or objectified. To honour someone is to hold dear to the boundary between yourself and another. Yet this boundary liberates people to love each other genuinely, not chase after others as vehicles for self-satisfaction.

The next three chapters shift gear to more societal concerns, beginning in Chapter 5, 'Obligation', with a critique of what might be grandly termed the epistemology of identity politics. Drawing particularly on the hermeneutical philosophy of Wilhelm Dilthey, I argue that the distinctive intellectual activities of the humanities (most fundamentally, interpretation) are structurally different to the natural sciences because of an inherent twofold structure of obligation. That is, to interpret something requires taking heed of a mutual obligation to subjectivity and objectivity. Natural science as classically understood adheres only to the obligation of objectivity. Yet, much of today's discourse on the humanities breaks the binary in the other direction, claiming all is subjectivity. Moreover, older approaches to the humanities argued that these disciplines just reflected the way people actually live. In life, we perpetually seek objective truth in a way that is properly integrated with subjectivity. Basic human cognition serves both masters.

Chapter 6, 'Respect', I wrote with great hesitation, as it entailed going into some of the most vexatious territory of contemporary society: race. The thesis here is that most discourse around race-relations, particularly since 2020, has drawn on American racial discourse, despite the fact that that discourse is often ill-fitted to a UK context. The effect of unconscious bias training sessions, for example, is to try to leverage respect between different ethnicities artificially and often in a way disconnected from the lived realities in which particular ethnicities have forged a particular shared culture in Britain for decades. This is not a pluralist multiculturalism I have in mind, but something much harder to achieve – mutual participation in a culture that is shared. I contrast the mutual, organic respect that is won by sharing a culture with the forced, artificial respect associated with terms like 'allyship', which are themselves often used by people who haven't lived within a shared culture themselves.

Chapter 7, 'Responsibility', discusses ecological concerns as expressed in the 1990s compared to the present day. Between the two periods, another broken binary has emerged – between cultural and social conservation and environmental conservation. This break is intensifying rapidly, with the current vogue for language of crisis and emergency pushing towards a near-permanent state-of-exception, radically disconnected from the past. But we need not go too far back in history to see how nature and culture were much more closely related than they are today.

The book then shifts gear again for the final three chapters, turning to even broader questions about language, the cosmos and, finally, authority. Chapter 8, 'Discipline', finds the epitome of the interrelation of obedience and freedom in poetics. Poetry is held to be writing freed from even the normal strictures of language and yet the requirements of the form are traditionally much stricter than prose. The fact that language today so easily slips into a bureaucratic and managerial turn of phrase (or anti-poetics) is symptomatic of our inability to use discipline in service of freedom.

Chapter 9, 'Duty', continues in a literary vein, bringing the six-volume autofiction work *My Struggle* by Karl Ove Knausgaard into dialogue with the differing cosmologies of the premodern, modern and postmodern periods. This chapter presents the view that premodern cosmology had a sense of duty 'hardwired' into it, not least due to its inherently God-centred structure, which was not entirely forsaken in the modern era. Knausgaard's work gives voice to premodern and modern impulses, stubbornly resisting the collapse into cosmic nihilism associated with postmodernity – particularly when he is in everyday situations of duty, such as caring for the young.

The book closes in Chapter 10 with a theme that surely sums up all those covered thus far: 'Authority'. This broken binary is perhaps the most important in showing how obedience perpetuates freedom, the degree to which it is indistinguishable from it, and vice versa. What many consider obedience today is just blind subjection, which is why there is some truth behind contemporary unease about the term. Similarly, what many people consider authority today is just an exertion of power, which supervenes over assent, again helping to explain why it has become a debased term. This chapter seeks to show that genuine obedience always involves a measure of assent and the genuine expression of authority has no need for the exertion of the power. However difficult it is for us to envisage this now, the interrelation of obedience and authority once stemmed from self-evidence, from the unquestioned conviction that those in authority were mandated to their position. Today's various 'contractual' forms of obedience effectively undermine authority and tend to get ensnared in individual desires, as indeed authority founded on just brute force undermines obedience and tends to unleash chaos.

The final scene of the book describes the notorious eviction of an illegal party on the Isle of Dogs in 1992. In the heat of the moment, the battle scene was indistinguishable from a dance, just as in today's world the culture wars are a form of recreation and entertainment, particularly on social media. Each set of opponents in that battle considered themselves sworn enemies. I argue that they were actually on the same side, unwittingly, just as those who want to resist all authority often end up in a grimly restrained manner of living and those who celebrate subjection slip into anarchic and antinomian lifestyles. In the small hours of the night, for a few short moments, the effects of this broken binary came together on the dancefloor in a field in a mysterious enclave of east London. From that moment we can glimpse what healing such binaries will entail. That is, that obedience is freedom.

1

Allegiance

An area of common land in West Berkshire lies near an intersection between the industrial cities of the Midlands to the north and the ports on the English Channel to the south. The same spot is intersected lengthways too, connecting west and east on the old horse-drawn carriage route between London and Bath. The common land is a few square miles of woodland, heath and scrub. For centuries it would hardly merit much attention. Being common land it has no explicit purpose as such; it is simply 'there'. But this land is also itself the site of an intersection of a different type. This land has a distinct history as a place on the intersection of war and peace.

This is documented from the time of the English Civil War. In 1643, Parliamentarian troops paused there to ready themselves for what was to be a decisive battle of that conflict. There are traces of much older earthworks still perceptible beneath the soil too. Long, linear banks of earth dated to the fifth century may have served a purpose for Roman troops, as even the circular Bronze Age pits nearby could have been used by a tribe practising with their weaponry before setting off to defend their settlements. It is said this site was later an outpost for soldiers preparing to defend Anglo-Saxon Silchester from attack. A map from 1740 shows a military camp set up there and in 1746 this camp was the base for despatching troops for battle with Bonny Prince Charlie. By 1859 it was being used as a training camp to prepare for a French invasion. There were 16,000 troops stationed there in 1862; in 1872, it was 20,000. Later it was used for infantry training for those going to the Western Front and eventually it was taken over by the Ministry of Defence for use as an airbase for the Second World War in 1941.

The history of this common land is given over fully neither to peace nor war; it is where they meet. This is where peacetime prepares for war. The order and obedience required for battle are established here. Yet this is also where fighters return to recuperate in peace, free from the demands of the fray. This is then a place of rest and regeneration.

A decisive change came some decades after the Second World War. This could be when the history of this place reaches a crescendo, when the meeting point between war and peace is suddenly brought into focus. People will then see this as a place that discloses that which is held in common by war and peace. For even winners and losers belong together. Both sides play the game. Both enter the scene, take the risk, yearn for the prize. To attempt to win the battle is to consent to possibly losing the battle. To enter into war is to accept you might not have peace on your terms. There is common ground between sides, in that each side shares something fundamental with the other. This is something beneath the battle itself, functioning like the rules of a game, tacitly present – just 'there' – like common land itself.

War and peace require a specific place of meeting if they are to be differentiated from one another. If times of war cannot become times of peace, the battle will never cease. Then, even in peacetime, everyone is at war. Recreation is riven with contention, people mistake combat for contentment. Order and obedience no longer intersect with rest and regeneration, because there is no boundary where you pass from one into the other. With no common ground from whence to be despatched into the heat of battle, there is no common ground to which to return and rest in the cool shade. War becomes cold war. Peacetime becomes intensely heated. Those who would feel the rush of victory can only do so if others are to feel the sorrow of defeat. There must be commonality from which each side departs, but also to which each side can return. In this belonging, obedience meets freedom.

The decisive change in the destiny of the common land came with the Cold War. NATO announced they would deploy cruise missiles in Europe on 12 December 1979. In 1981, it was reported that these missiles would be housed on two sites in England, one of which was this common land. It would provide a base from which military trucks could depart carrying these missiles if or when they were launched at important cities in the Soviet Bloc. The missiles were to be kept in large concrete silos, six in number. These resemble ancient ziggurats or pyramids, with heavy shutters opening to vast chambers, where their precious cargo would be immersed in the deep darkness within. It is difficult for us fully to appreciate how sinister these seemingly sentient missiles seemed in an age less technological than our own. They were remotely controlled and could fly a thousand miles below the flight radars. Each one contained enough atomic power to detonate an explosion sixteen times the size of Hiroshima. The spark of Prometheus lay nascent within each silo, ready for the floods to break forth upon the Earth when the shutters opened.

In a pamphlet from the early 1980s, a mother in a nearby town describes the moment this new purpose for this local land was announced on the news:

> I had seen a BBC TV programme about nuclear war . . . It came to the bit about putting dead bodies in plastic bags with labels on and leaving them in the road to be collected. I sat in front of the television, my one-year-old in my arms, my heart sinking with fear. Someone, somewhere, is actually accepting the fact that my children will die. Someone, somewhere, is quietly planning for the deaths of millions. This is not a dream, it is real.[1]

This mother became one of many thousands of women who protested against the cruise missiles base in the years that followed. She had joined with others in organizing a march from a nuclear weapon's facility in Cardiff to the common land and the scenes that followed are those with which this common land is now always associated: Greenham Common.

Initially they called themselves 'Women for Life on Earth'. Leaving Cardiff on 27 August, they arrived on 5 September: 'a long straggling line of women and children tramping through the dusty Berkshire lanes with leaves in their hair'.[2] The single-carriage roads that led up to the site were arched over by the boughs of ancient trees, under which far more orderly battalions had once marched in lockstep. The woodland on either side was birthing its September fruits. The leaves were still green and lush, just tinged by the encroaching autumn.

When nature called, the kids would run ahead and duck under these trees, clambering through the leaves into dusty enclosures enclosed by broad, low branches. Some would dare to run further into the woods, wanting to be first to glimpse the eight-foot wire fence recently erected around the Common. On the other side of this fence, the grass had that scorched yellow colour that can make the English countryside in late August feel almost Mediterranean, if only for a few long days. Squinting in the summer sun after emerging from the trees, the kids saw freshly tarmacked roads and a few clusters of USAF buildings in the distance. The marchers emerged from the mysterious hollows and reaches of the English countryside to approach the main gate. Mowed grass verges appeared, with gorse between them and the woods, and neatly trimmed little privet hedges in front. Coming from the musty darkness of the trees into the brightly dazzling sun, the newly landscaped terrain seemed fuzzy and unreal.

There was a carnival atmosphere. The women had a folk band playing alongside them and 'they all looked so beautiful with their scarves and ribbons and flowers . . . The colours, the beauty, the sun . . . and so many people'.[3] Some had decided to chain themselves to the fences and maybe it was the joyful intensity of the occasion that led some of the others to decide they could not simply go back home and return to normal. Some set up a large campfire and slept out under the stars. Over the following days provisions arrived, makeshift structures were erected and, around the nucleus of the fire, some of the women decided to stay indefinitely. The encampment was later named Greenham Common Women's Peace Camp. Over the next three years it developed into what is now a well-known chapter in recent English history.

Within a few weeks it was decided it should be a women-only space. Some of the men present had been confrontational with the authorities, taken control of elements of the camp, or been overprotective of the women during skirmishes with bailiffs and police. These behaviours were not welcome. Numerous direct actions, court cases, imprisonments and campaigns took place in the next three years. The most well-known event is probably the 'Embrace the Base' event on 11 December 1983, when 30,000 women encircled and enclosed the entire base, linking arms around the nine-mile perimeter fence. There were marquees set up by the main gate for refreshments and childcare. The kids inside were kept amused with painting and make-shift puppet shows and their creations were later used to decorate the barbed wire. The event was on national television news. During the report, talking heads were interviewed in front of the main gate, voicing either approval or disapproval of the action. The kids' brightly coloured paintings and puppets could be seen some way behind them but the wire fence was not visible at such a distance. Their creations thus seemed to be suspended in mid-air, hovering on the horizon. The women's children, seeing their pictures on the TV, would be overcome with excitement and pride. Their triumphant cheers drowned out the droning commentary on the merits or demerits of the event itself.

Other direct actions were more volatile, taking place under cover of darkness. The project to house cruise missiles at USAF Greenham Common involved regular manoeuvres, when military trucks would take the missiles out of the silos and drive them around the sur-rounding countryside of Hampshire and Wiltshire, usually to a firing range on Salisbury Plain, five miles west of Stonehenge. To prepare and practise for a launch, the missiles would be edged out of the Greenham silos with great care, with much monitoring, pacing and controlled moments of focused pushing. Then the warheads left their dark place and were exposed for a moment to the night air and the stars, before being bundled hastily into the cribs built onto the mil-itary trucks waiting outside. These nuclei of awesome atomic power were then borne along the country lanes, passing through the high streets of small local towns, around the market squares and past the pubs, newsagents and grocery shops.

The women had phone networks on 24-hour alert all around the surrounding counties and would mount spontaneous blockades and sit-ins on the country lanes to stop these manoeuvres. These block-ades developed into liturgies with regular features; sometimes the lighting of flares or the smearing of mud on the trucks' windscreens while the convoy waited for police to clear the roads. Often, the operation would be aborted and the missiles sent back in retreat. Returning to the Common, the ancient role of Greenham would then recommence. This was always a site of both exit and return; a place from which people could depart into battle, but also come back to peace. The missiles went from *ex utero* to *in utero*. The shutters would be reopened, the cargo carefully laid back in the immersive darkness. As the soldiers trekked back to their lodgings shortly before dawn, they would hear the triumphant women drinking and singing in victory around the dots of flame they could make out coming from their fires all along the perimeter fence. With each battle's end, there was a common place to which people returned.

The Women's Peace Camp was a nexus of intersecting battlelines. There was the intersection of west and east. This was the making local in parochial England of the architectonic power blocks of the Cold War. This was where the opposition of the 'free world' to 'communism' was not rhetorical, it was real. It was also where the faultlines in domestic politics met, still then largely categorizable as Left and Right. The actual battles of the Cold War were never really between Americans and Russians, nor did the Greenham Women interact much with the American troops who worked in the compound. When there was combat, it was between fellow citizens, between the protestors and the police or bailiffs, or between others sympathetic to either one side or another. One woman described the locals of Greenham with contempt as exuding a 'kind of deferential, cap-touching Toryism'.[4] The villagers were angry about the encampment, as were many of their magistrates, councillors and judges. Stories were passed from woman to woman along the pathways encircling the base, of local men lurking in the brambles ready to pounce or gangs of lads pouring sacks of cement into their tanks of drinking water. Even among the women various tensions flared up, usually between those with more radical and separatist impulses, against those with careers, husbands and children to factor into their plans. Yet another battleline surrounded the camp; that between men and women. This is the most primordial division of them all, a boundary always assumed until recently to be the most insurmountable.

Looking at this episode of history now, certain things command our attention. The command is heard all the more forcefully because the official chroniclers of Greenham have been so inattentive. Looking at history with your eyes firmly focused upon it makes your own time look different when your gaze turns back. Glance at history lazily and your eyes will never see the horizon beyond your own. Then history affirms the status quo, the boundary between then and now is just as expected, not fuzzy and unreal as your eyes adjust to something new. But Greenham does not just ratify the values of today, there are times when it also revokes them. That is, this episode shows a clear intersecting of things today's culture wars cannot countenance as belonging together.

Today's identitarian feminists would struggle particularly with Greenham's celebration of natality, of the primordial commonality between mother and child. Those who hold that defining womanhood through life-giving capacities is but an outdated remnant of obedience to the patriarchy only see things from the other side of a broken binary. Their eyes cannot be focused on those moments when such things were held in common. If the duties of motherhood are always enslaving, women's liberation is freedom from procreation. But, to look attentively means that behind the permitted voices hover the remnants of very different experiences – suspended along the horizon, out of focus, some distance away – the wire fences holding our contemporary maladies in place disappear, leaving only the colourful expressions of a more innocent time. Greenham is striking today because many of these women went into battle precisely because they saw themselves as the handmaidens of life on Earth, by virtue of being women.

The quote given above from a mother moved to political activism after she was 'sat in front of the television, my one-year-old in my arms, my heart sinking with fear' is but one example. The bind between mother and infant unbinds her energies to be expressed in political action. The name 'Women for Life on Earth' would today seem more natural for a pro-life group than a feminist organization. The similarities do not end here. One of the original leaflets for this group asks 'Why are we walking 120 miles from a nuclear weapon facility in Cardiff to a site for Cruise missiles in Berkshire?' On the back was a picture of a baby born dead, killed by the radiation from

Hiroshima, saying 'This is why.'[5] At least one key player in setting up the camp was a midwife. Welcoming and integrating mothers with children and babies was a *sine qua non* of it being a space for women, a place where the demands of motherhood could be genuinely welcomed by those upon whom such demands are ever laid.

Natality informed the rationale for a distinctively women's peace movement: 'because I am a woman I am responsible', said one.[6] Dora Russell wrote that peacemaking is a natural extension of a feminine genius: 'If differences are not to be settled by war but by negotiation, there must be more feeling for cooperation', she says, and '[w]ithin a family, a wife and mother traditionally tries to reconcile differences'.[7] She points out that there was a broad spectrum involved in the movement, including some who, like today's dominant voices, considered a focus on procreative capacities to be symptomatic of male oppression. But this doesn't detract from the fact that keeping our eyes firmly fixed on this episode makes it clear that a great many involved in Greenham Common would be unwelcome in feminist political activism today. They would be cancelled and endlessly trolled as conservatives or reactionaries.

This side to Greenham is a story very few of its contemporary admirers are likely to tell. But, as Russell stated in 1983, 'there are large numbers of women who felt compelled to act *because* of the traditional roles in which they found themselves'.[8] The group Babies Against the Bomb was founded by Tamar Swade, who describes early motherhood as joining 'a separate species of two-legged, four-wheeled creatures who carry their young in push-chair pouches' and who occasionally 'converged for a "coffee morning" or a mother-and-baby group run by the National Childbirth Trust'. At these gatherings, there would be 'much discussion about nappy-rash, (not) sleeping and other problems pertaining to the day-to-day survival of mother and infant'. The thinking behind Babies Against the Bomb led directly from these most motherly of concerns – 'Why not start a mother-and-baby group whose discussions included *long-term* survival?' she asks. For '[t]hrough my child the immorality of this world . . . has become intolerable'.[9]

Understandings of womanhood in the world of Greenham, closely linked to femininity as procreative, cannot be explained away as internalized patriarchy or the unfortunate residue of past oppressions that we have now progressed beyond. It is difficult to imagine the Greenham Women responding positively if asked to redefine their women-only space in such a way that procreation is no longer inextricably bound up with their identity as women. Yet it is easy to imagine how the online discourse would condemn them as right-wing, religious cranks for having the audacity to set up what some might insist is renamed a 'People with Uteruses Peace Camp'. Once these remnants of the past have come clearly into view, the horizon of the present is then altered. Today's world starts to seem fuzzy and unreal.

There is real a sense of freedom documented by these women who would not consider motherhood mere subservience, freedom from a gynophobic capitalism, which pushed motherhood to the periphery, away from the purportedly more serious, male-dominated workplace. The women's bind to their infants – their unquestioning allegiance to their children – freed them from the inexorable self-centredness that prevents people from taking responsibility for the wellbeing of others. Once a binary is broken, differentiation is lost because the other side falls out of view. Viewing natality as subservience lapses into a surreptitious totalitarianism. Contemporary society values transience, optionality, re-invention. It fears permanent, unconditional attachment like that of parent and child. Then, living in a culture that dismisses unconditional attachment leaves people conditioned by self-attachment. The drive for self-fulfilment dominates. Disparaging the love more visceral than any other fosters a culture that is less responsible in ways extending far beyond child-rearing itself. A culture in which child-bearing is conditional on self-fulfilment is restrained from developing basic impulses of responsibility and care throughout. This is not to say that only those who have children exercise such responsibilities. It is to say that the degree to which natality is celebrated in a culture is a vital barometer of how responsible that culture is. Obediently accepting the demand of allegiance promises a more genuine freedom, more genuine than that pseudo-freedom that leaves people locked up in themselves.

Seen in this light, it is important not to explain away the inextricability of motherhood and womanhood for Greenham. It is spoken of as

something that fostered solidarity between the women. Bodily repro-
duction, potential or actual, was assumed to be primarily a matter for
women, something in which men participate in a very different way. It
was not the only touchstone of solidarity, of course. Others included
the threat or experience of sexual violence, particularly. This is always
lurking in the songs, poems and writings of the women, like the
legends of local men peering at them from beneath the brambles, and
is often bound up with allusions to domestic circumstances, which
led some of the women to 'up sticks' and live on the camp in the first
place. But men *can* be victims of sexual violence, albeit far less often,
with far fewer cultural apologias and never fostering male solidarity.
Bearing the locus of the generation of life in conception, however,
and gestating that life, giving birth to it and then suckling it – these
were then implicitly assumed to be things men could not possibly do,
without question. The exclusive priority of this allegiance of a mother
to her child, over all else, meant that women, particularly, felt called
to protest against the threat of nuclear war.

For the threat of nuclear war felt terrible to those who had recently
borne children into the world. Swade discusses one who was compelled to join the Peace Movement because 'the mention of nuclear
war conjures the waking nightmare of her children burning'. Another
describes a recurring dream in which 'the four-minute warning would
come while she was at work' so she couldn't 'cross town in time' to
get to her offspring.[10] One woman, Simone Wilkinson, connects her
decision to join the first march with an encounter she had with a
Japanese woman, while pregnant with her second child. She was told
that 'when a woman was pregnant in Hiroshima, she was given no
congratulations but people waited in silence for nine months until the
child was born, to see if it was all right'.[11] Swade describes the new-
born baby as a 'creature whose every impulse is towards survival but
who is so dependent for it upon others'. She goes on, 'my immediate,
instinctive reaction to nuclear war is in my capacity as a mother'.[12]
The intensity of this inter-human dependence in motherly instincts
thus fostered a belonging with any others under threat of nuclear war.

If motherhood could foster the wide-ranging concern for others
that drove anti-nuclear protesting, it could even foster a belonging

between the two sides that did actually enter into battle. These are the opposing sets of citizens; the women and their opponents in society at large.

For example, the campfires burned at Greenham throughout the Falklands War. Battlelines intersected between the Peace Movement and those celebrating the 'Gotcha!' jingoism of 'Our Lads' vs 'the Argies'. On 12 October 1982 there was a victory parade for the returning troops in London. A group of women decided to go, turn their backs on the parade as it passed them and unfurl a banner saying 'Women Turn Their Backs on War'. An account of this action by Lynne Jones presents it as something not intended to be overly confrontational, as such. She says that the victory in the Falklands was a victory also for British 'democratic liberties' and these were lacking in Argentina, so the jubilant crowds could be expected to support that freedom of expression at the parade. Having found a spot along the route, Jones and her group of activists waited incognito among the people with their Union Jacks. She got talking to a mother of one of the returning soldiers. She addresses her account to this woman directly: 'A plump, smiling woman, your hair freshly done, bright blue eyes, who came and stood right in the middle of our group.' She goes on: 'You chose us deliberately, you told me, because we weren't too tall and you thought you could get a good view over our shoulders.'

They ended up talking a lot as they waited and the disguised Peace Woman helped the military mother with working her new camera. It had just been purchased so the mother could catch a memento of the proud moment her boy marched past with his regiment. Jones mentions a connection between each of the women, centred on motherhood: 'Here you were, in your best clothes, come a long way with your husband to see your son who'd got home safe from war' and 'Here was I, equally glad your son was safe.' This motherly connection came to a head when the action began and the women unfurled their banner and turned their backs on the soldiers. There was a commotion, with jeers and insults thrown at the women, one of whom broke down in tears at seeing the horrified reaction from their new blue-eyed friend. The military mother cried out, 'I thought you cared about my son!' The Peace Woman replied 'It's because we care about your son that we're here!' The old common land of Greenham was at that moment active in the heart of the capital city. In that moment both sides saw they were coming from the same place, the same set of motherly concerns, they just differed on how those concerns should be realized.

Jones reflects further on what the two women held in common. She writes: 'We share the same values, you and I. We love freedom and happiness.' Then she turns to where the difference lay: 'You would tell me such things can only be maintained because your son fights to protect them'; whereas she would say, 'The fact he has to fight destroys the things themselves.'[13] This last observation is important. According to this account there is a profound commonality between the women, not just as mothers, but also as each bearing an allegiance to a particular cultural sensibility and set of assumptions described in terms of 'freedom and happiness'. The difference between them centres on how best to realize and achieve the manner of life they both want. There is common ground, it is just 'there'. The differentiation is not a broken binary, because neither side refuses to countenance the opposing position. This holds the promise that there is somewhere they can meet, that this particular battle can eventually cease.

It is hard to imagine such an account emerging from the battles of today's culture war. That is, from the moment, say, a man appeared from nowhere in Parliament Square during the Black Lives Matter protest of 2020 and ripped down all the racial slogans from Churchill's statue, or when a youth was stopped from setting fire to the Union Jack on the Cenotaph later that day. Neither are there any such accounts from the annual Women Against Trump marches each January nor the 'MAGA stand-off' between Nathan Phillips and the protesting teenagers at March for Life. One of the most active protest groups, Extinction Rebellion, employs a rhetorical framework which means common ground is impossible to reach; there can be no accommodation to human extinction. All this shows that the culture war is fought on the other side of a broken binary, the common ground is no longer just 'there'.

Once the common ground has gone, war and peace can no longer be distinguished. A war among cultures is the coldest of wars. Insofar as culture is defined as 'a whole way of life',[14] to war against another culture is to enter into battle against a foe with whom there is no common ground. That is, no acceptance of a shared origin or history that can be agreed upon, no acceptance of a shared endeavour to realize and perpetuate in a common manner of living and no ultimate ends or goals to which a shared culture might lead people. A war like this, not centred on physical combat, can be enslaving in all dimensions of life. Even those not conscripted into battle are still restrained from engaging with challenging ideas because the dominant side deems them toxic. Being on the other side of broken binary means people of different views are treated with suspicion and distrust. For those who do engage with the war directly, notifications ping from social media late in the small hours of the night, invading every private space and all domesticity. There is no place to which one can retreat, nowhere to return and be recuperated. Common land, like Wendell Berry says of wilderness, belongs to 'nobody' and so 'belongs to everybody', it is 'the natural enmity of tyranny'.[15]

A shared common ground of belonging, of mutual allegiance, functions like a womb from which society and culture come forth. A culture that is estranged from natality betokens a culture suspicious of mutual allegiance at its most visceral. A culture thus truncated is condemned always to be fractious, always ensnared in unbridgeable differences of opinion. A culture that celebrates primordial allegiance, however, can know the freedom of shared endeavour. As Christopher Lasch states, 'the sources of social cohesion' are to be found 'in shared assumptions so deeply engrained in everyday life that they don't have to be articulated: in folkways, customs, prejudices, habits of the heart'.[16] This source or origin was once simply 'there'; the tacit, unspoken assumption that each belonged to and came from a particular place, to which they would always return once hostilities had settled. It functions like that Paul Embery describes an 'old universal moral code', binding on all, 'irrespective' of 'class or political beliefs'; a 'deep social and cultural homogeneity', which engenders 'a spirit of reciprocity and belonging'.[17]

In this substratum of allegiance, we encounter identity unpoliticized, not intersected by ideological commitments, something more primary than the political. To make identity fundamentally political is to drag the unspoken realm of our 'habits of the heart' into the harsh light of day. That which sleeps within is then always awoken. People are rendered 'woke'. To be woke is to have lost the place of inward slumber and not to know one's way back to it. One is not 'awake' because the present needs to grow from the past to be truly present. Instead, the alienated past lingers on and torments the present and so the word has slipped into the past tense. Being woke means to be deprived of a past, to be living in a tortuously enduring state of having always just-this-second awoken. It is to live in those dread infinitesimal first milliseconds of the morning, before you can remember the day before or what lies in store for the day ahead. It is to be disorientated, unkempt and squinting under the merciless strip lights of a world that aborts itself in every moment. It is no coincidence that the Jacobins declared Year 1 after the French Revolution or that the agitators at the barricades in 1851 dated all their correspondence from that date for the rest of their lives. To call something 'progressive' is to secure a vantage for the present that rudely cuts out the past.

The *Guardian* songbook of Greenham Common prints the lyrics of one of the camp's most common songs: 'Carry Greenham Home'. Those who celebrate this music today do not notice how haunting it is, because this period of history still evinces the sense of a shared cultural home, of mutual allegiance. Then, shared concerns could be expressed differently and contentiously, while still remaining shared. This allegiance resides not in the sphere of conscious assent, of self-chosen lifestyles or desired identities. A culture truncated from its sources of social cohesion is perpetually *ex utero*, forever orphaned, because it is deprived of that which lies beyond any choosing or self-selection, of that 'so deeply engrained in everyday life' it does not 'have to be articulated'. This is also why it is so hard to imagine a way back, because that would be a way to go from *ex utero* to *in utero*. This also explains why the phrase 'culture war' is ubiquitous and yet the phrase 'culture peace' has not yet been coined. There is a broken binary and repair is needed if we are ever to envisage a *pax cultura*.

The generative promise of mutual allegiance seems fuzzy and unreal to us today. It is jarring to suggest that what people think of as inhibitive of freedom actually liberates people to be themselves. It is counter-intuitive to say that dutiful attachments actually free people to live their lives fully. Looking back on this antiquated viewpoint is like being the man who was once that one-year-old on his mother's lap when the news about the cruise missile base went out on TV. It feels fuzzy and unreal to read about yourself as a babe in arms, stumbling across this passage as an adult many years later. This describes a moment deeply engrained in my own history, yet I am not even aware of it at all. It lies somewhere beyond my conscious awareness. It is beyond my memories; beyond my earliest reminiscences of skipping through the woodland around the common on a summer's day; beyond my remembering of the triumphant cheer I voiced when my childlike painting was shown on the national news on a December night. But all of us were once caught up in an allegiance like that my mother described in that passage. Our allegiance to peoples and places similarly sleeps somewhere within us and seems unreal to us now. But this is not a dream, this is real.

2

Loyalty

The scene of exclusive allegiance between mother and child is dream-like, for it lies somewhere within the deepest recesses of my own consciousness. But it pertains to only one side of a coin, the other side of which is etched permanently on every facet of my conscious life. To do justice to this other side would mean writing a book longer than this one and even then it would only skim the surface. Some years after my mother relayed that moment during which my one-year-old self slept in her arms, she became gravely ill and underwent a profound physical and mental deterioration, which steadily worsened over the course of twenty years.

I was sixteen when she became ill. The doctors had various hypotheses as to what might have caused it, but months of unpleasant procedures and stays in hospitals only made the symptoms worse. It seemed to be some kind of brain injury, they said. When I first saw her after it had happened, something had changed. I could not at that age articulate this change in my own thoughts, save for a vague sense of panic when I noticed it, or noticed the degradation of her appearance that came with it. Her hopes of returning to work were abandoned after a couple of attempts left her rushing home in a taxi, incapacitated for days afterwards. Within a couple of years she gave up on the medical establishment completely. She spent considerable sums on alternative therapies, none of which made any difference. The decline only ever got steadily, assuredly worse.

By my early twenties, my mother was completely housebound. I'd long since moved out, but I went over a couple of times of week to do her shopping and take the bins out. Her home was decaying around her. The responsibility was at times difficult to bear. It dictated where I went to university, where I lived, my career choices. I'd get exasperated by the frequent crises requiring emergency visits due to broken appliances and utilities. My mother would only accept help from me; she always resisted any external support or assistance. For most of a period of twenty years I was the only person she spoke with. I was her sole human interaction: once or twice a week, for two decades. Eventually her physical and mental decline posed such a threat to her safety that she accepted the need to move to a situation of full-time care. She died five weeks later.

From the age of sixteen to thirty-five, I was affected by this situation in various ways. When I spoke of it, people's reactions fell into one of two types or, more commonly, veered from one into the other. This took the form of, firstly, cheap, superficial epi-thets like: 'That's very good of you to look after her.' Then, secondly, less cheap and often quite considered soundings about 'letting go', 'stepping back', 'looking after yourself', 'being wary of another person's "baggage"' and so on. There was certainly some wisdom in this second response. Being a carer can be fraught with co-dependent behaviours. But what interests me is how these two reactions were disconnected with one another and often self-contradictory. In what way was it 'very good of me' to be a carer, if it was also deemed good (or, usually better) to walk away? People seemed to assume I was trapped between trying to do right by my mother and wanting to do right by myself. There was a stand-off in people's responses: between being obedient ('the right thing to do') and being free ('walk away'). The latter option certainly invoked the most passionate responses.

I sometimes asked myself what advice I would have been given twenty, fifty or a hundred years previously. Surely, caring for an elderly or unwell relative was once considered primarily in terms of being 'the right thing to do' and not an infringement of realizing one's potential. I knew full well the thinking behind both responses. I knew full well it might be deemed a noble thing to do. I equally knew full well it meant I could not do other things that I'd be free to do otherwise, things I desperately wanted to do. What I needed was the ability to join these two responses into one, a way out of the aporia. I needed to be free enough to do what was asked of me by the situation I was in, to be free to stay put. But the freedom of which people spoke was only freedom to make something more of myself, never the freedom to stand in the midst of circumstances I would never have chosen.

The attitudes a particular culture demonstrates towards childbirth and child-rearing are indicative of a much broader neuralgia about shared responsibilities and mutual allegiance. The attitudes a culture exhibits to the care of the elderly and unwell are no less significant. Indeed, the situation is surely even worse, as can be seen by the 'care crisis' and ongoing debates about ageing populations. The root issue here is culture. The numbers of elderly or ailing parents in care homes is much higher in those cultures of a more individualistic bent, particularly Britain, the United States and Germany. Just as with allegiance in natality, an obedient acceptance of the loyalty people can bear for others would bespeak a culture where belonging is not merely conditional on personal choice, on what is deemed to suit one's own best interests, disconnected from others.

The freedom to stand alongside others when it goes against one's own choosing is what it means to be genuinely loyal. Such loyalty can sometimes involve standing alongside those undeserving of your fidelity, because they are just 'there', proximate to you. Viewed socially, this would mean loyalty to one's cultural setting, in a way not dictated by ideological alignment. This is something that references to loyalty today often sidestep, assuming it is secondary to choice – deciding first that you agree with some cause and then choosing to be loyal to it. That is, ultimately reducing belonging to a matter of self-chosen identity, to ideology or politics. Sometimes there seems to be no way back from here, no way to imagine a sense of loyalty to a shared cultural identity, which is more fundamental than individual free will.

Helen Andrews states: 'Old-fashioned virtues like loyalty not only aren't practised; they are no longer considered virtues.' People are permitted to 'be loyal to an institution – employer, school, your country of birth – to the extent that it conforms to your values and not one iota more'.[1] Steadfast dedication, even to something with which we disagree, is today likely to be seen as being held captive, as sheer unfreedom. But limiting loyalty only to that which aligns with our whims and desires is to limit it to that which is transient, thus rendering it not real loyalty at all. Values change. We do not choose our parents on the basis of their political opinions. Limiting loyalty only to what conforms to your values is what restrains.

We need to understand how we got to where we are today, to envisage how we might find our way back to being loyal. Today's climate of what Christopher Lasch calls the 'balkanization of opinion' has followed the politicization of identity.[2] What Paul Embery describes as a 'deep social and cultural homogeneity', which engenders 'a spirit of reciprocity and belonging', by contrast, is identity un-politicized; identity as a primordial reality more fundamental than political choices and preferences. Jonathan Haidt's *The Righteous Mind* offers one attempt to find out how things have gone so awry. Haidt seeks to understand why 'good people are divided by religion and politics'. He charts his own intellectual development from the influence of liberal 'rationalists', which dictated that people 'figure out morality for themselves' rather than simply carry within them a morality of their culture that commands loyalty.[3] He discusses how Elliot Turiel claimed to show that children could differentiate social conventions, that is, 'rules about clothing, food and many other aspects of life' from moral rules, such as those which prevent harm. Being loyal pertains to the realm of convention, to circumstances Turiel would deem arbitrary. 'Moral development', however, was seen by Turiel as individual self-realization, as unshackling oneself from loyalty by discerning the parameters of 'harm and fairness'. This purportedly moral rationality was seen as working against the binds of 'loyalty, respect, duty, piety, patriotism or tradition'.[4]

Such 'rationalism' holds that loyalty must be treated with suspicion, for to consider being loyal as intrinsically good threatens to confuse what is right or wrong with mere accidents of birth. To his credit, Haidt recognizes that things are not so simple. He defines two sets of concerns – one rooted in belonging, allegiance and loyalty and the other in rationally discerned universality – as pertaining to 'two different kinds of cognition: intuition and reasoning'. The intuitive is the realm of instinct and reasoning is about the 'controlled processes' of premises and conclusions. He hopes this insight could help diffuse the warring factions in American society, who are typically

Republicans and Democrats. He maintains that it is not that one side believes in allegiance ('loyalty, respect, duty, piety, patriotism or tradition') and the other in non-allegiance (the universality of 'harm and fairness'), but rather that everyone has, to use his metaphor, differently arranged 'taste receptors', giving differing degrees of influence to different forms of cognition. That is, everyone needs to be loyal to some extent, just as everyone can discern universally valid rules about avoiding harm. The issue is how those degrees of concern differ in different people.

Haidt's primary metaphor concerns 'riders and elephants'. The rider works by 'reasoning why' the moral status of something is how it is, which leads to universal principles of right and wrong, untethered from local allegiances. The elephant works by 'seeing that' something is the way it is, not as a reasoned conclusion, but as something simply 'there', to which it is inextricably linked.[5] During moments of conflict, elephants will not listen to reason. The person whose group allegiance blinds them to, say, an atrocity committed by their side in war will not be convinced that the action was unjustified because their loyalty holds sway. Elephants are not easily steered by their riders; they like to take back control. 'We are deeply intuitive creatures whose gut feelings drive our strategic reasoning.' This means mere 'reasoning why' won't turn everyone into cosmopolitan liberals. We all have the faculty for such reasoning, but it is more often than not put into the service of our prior commitments. Then it works to justify the instincts in those for whom the prior commitments are strong. Mere reasoning will not undermine their loyalty.

Haidt maintains that his metaphors of 'taste receptors' and 'elephants and riders' should be put into service for creating an atmosphere of 'affection' and 'admiration' between the two sides, which are ultimately the same in their humanity but just differ in their internal proportions. Respectful conduct towards those with dominant elephants will enable their elephants to change course, because their instinctual levels will be roused by the compassionately human face of the other side. He calls on Democrats not to assume 'that Republicans have duped these people into voting against their economic self-interest', but rather to remember that a different set of interests was activated by the Republican campaigns, namely 'their moral interests'; that is, their sense of loyalty to something they unreflectively assume to be good.[6]

Haidt's discussion of belonging highlights the fact that a significant regard for authority often goes along with it. He draws on Alan Fiske's findings that hierarchical relationships mirror those of a 'parent and child' rather than a 'dictator and formal underlings'. Haidt says this is why he stopped subscribing to the 'common liberal belief that hierarchy=power=exploitation=evil'. Fiske's primary example of legitimate hierarchy is the military. There, people 'have asymmetric positions in a linear hierarchy to which subordinates defer, respect and (perhaps) obey, while superiors take precedence and take personal responsibility for subordinates'. Like the relationships of traditional parenting, these hierarchies are based on 'legitimate asymmetries, not coercive power'.[7]

Acknowledging legitimate hierarchy is connected to the way Haidt draws on Durkheim's account of religion so as to critique New Atheism. New Atheists consider religious people to have erroneous beliefs and to thus commit highly dubious actions. For Durkheim, however, belonging, or religious allegiance, is as important as believing and doing, as important as the explicit creeds and manner of living that religious adherents undertake. Whether good and bad outcomes of religion arise, then, depends on the differing tenors of religious communities in which people are 'enmeshed in a set of norms, relationships and institutions'.[8] For Durkheim, religions offer 'binding foundations', which activate our receptors connected to allegiance: 'Loyalty, Authority and Sanctity'.[9] Belonging is not intrinsically dangerous, therefore. It depends on that to which we belong. Returning to the political realm, that Republicans feel a strong sense of belonging to the USA is not a problem. It only becomes a problem if that belonging blinds those voters to incidents of harm, when reason should take over. Those voters are only in a dangerous position if they will not reassess their position after seeing footage like that of Abu Ghraib prison, for example.

The dominant North American liberalism is critiqued by Haidt for presenting those who care most about their belonging as always wrongheaded. As an evolutionary psychologist, he locates the basis for this in primitive reflexes of the human mind. He suggests we imagine 'a small bump on the back of our heads – the live switch, just under the skin, waiting to be turned on', and this is the switch to 'group righteousness'. This exists for the perpetuation of the species; it was necessary in human evolution for people to want to defend their tribes or communities against all the odds.[10] But there are two problems with Haidt's analysis. In the first place, notwithstanding the great lengths he goes to to present those who cherish allegiance as not intrinsically inferior, there is a clear superiority on display in that he considers this allegiance to be 'primitive'. His imaginary 'switch' on the back of our heads would presumably be somewhere near that real bump on the rear of the cranium wherein lies our 'reptilian brain'. Here lie the functions that human beings share with other animals, regulating pulse, sexuality and respiration, reminding us of our most ancient origins in the slimy mud. By this approach, things like 'loyalty, respect, duty, piety, patriotism or tradition' are noble-sounding things, with their roots in very ignoble places. They are 'legitimate' in the same way defaecation is legitimate; undoubtedly necessary and unavoidable, but hardly something to be cherished and celebrated.

Secondly, while Haidt questions a moral critique of belonging per se, he unwittingly shifts that critique to an aspect of this belonging which is singled out as particularly problematic: loyalty. While he maintains it is not wrong to value allegiance, indeed we must all do this to some extent, the implication is that – when historical circumstances demand it – it is crucial to let your sense of allegiance be corrected by a regard for the avoidance of harm and for fairness. That is, the voter for George W. Bush who remained fanatically pro-USA in the aftermath of Abu Ghraib *is* morally problematic; he or she has committed the opposite error to the Democrat, who assumes all patriotic people are evil: the dominance of one set of 'taste-receptors' by another, in this case the 'belonging receptors'. Haidt thus leaves us with a legitimacy of belonging, but an approach to loyalty that is deeply suspicious.

If the 'balkanization of opinion' cannot be met by finding some de-balkanized region of our internal hardwiring, let us turn to somewhere external. David Goodhart was provoked to write his *Road to Somewhere* by concerns similar to Haidt's, but in a British context. He recognizes 'the great divide' as it has intensified after 2016, when 'the politics of culture and identity rose to challenge the politics of Left and Right'.[11] There is now a 'core values divide', he says, 'relating to order and authority', which 'cuts across age, income, education and even political parties in Western democracies': between *Anywheres* and *Somewheres*.[12] He sees one side as being led by their allegiance, the other as considering themselves to have progressed beyond it. His research does indeed show that the 'values divide' is deeply affected by people's situation with respect to this differentiation, between those who live within twenty miles of their place of origin, opposed to the 'mobile, graduate, upper professional elite'.[13]

Anywheres 'see the world from Anywhere', meaning they see people as 'rational, self-interested individuals existing apart from strong group attachments or loyalties'. Somewheres 'see the world from Somewhere', evincing 'strong local attachments' where belonging is constitutive of their worldview.[14] Talcott Parsons describes Anywheres as having 'achieved identities', where 'sense of worth' comes from 'education and career success'. By contrast, Somewheres have 'ascribed identities', which derive 'from bonds of place or group'.[15] By Goodhart's reckoning, the culture wars are about the 'value divergence' between these two types of citizen. The frustration of the Somewheres reached the ballot boxes during the Brexit referendum. Then, says Goodhart, the fact that 'for most people life has never been better' in terms of income was trumped by the fact that 'in other respects life really isn't better . . . in terms of belonging'.[16]

From this diagnosis of the problem, he proposes certain ways to fulfil 'the urgent task of finding a new settlement between two worldviews'.[17] This includes developing a revivified sense of national identity. He notes that 'most people with strong identification with a local community also have correspondingly strong national identities' and suggests that if Anywheres develop some sense of national belonging there could be common ground again.[18] This is to take shape through governmental policies and initiatives. The time has come, we read, for Anywheres to stop 'looking down on Somewheres' and 'even accommodate some of their sentiments and intuitions'.[19] The task is to provide 'a sense of national solidarity, of sharing a common fate' which can 'transcend' differences in values: a 'strong, confident national identity . . . provides a template, an idiom', which 'assumes certain shared norms and common interests'.[20] Goodhart argues that Anywheres should accept that both groups have concerns that 'are decent and legitimate'.[21] He thus calls for an 'emotionally intelligent Anywhere liberalism', which can accept the need for 'a strong sense of belonging and group attachment'.[22]

Goodhart thus argues for a 'combination' of the two sets of concerns. This takes shape in terms of a truce, treaty or settlement – what he calls a 'balance of forces'.[23] Aspects of 'Anywhere freedom and Somewhere rootedness' have 'got out of balance', he says, but the 'two halves of humanity's political soul' can be reconciled into a 'happier co-existence'.[24] By accepting the legitimacy of Somewhere concerns, he says, there can be toleration between the warring factions, which requires 'a less headstrong Anywhere liberalism'.[25]

Goodhart's analysis is compelling and his analysis has gained in credibility since the collapse of the Labour vote in the Red Wall constituencies in 2019, as well as the discussions surrounding the Conservative victory in the Hartlepool by-election in 2021. These events are commonly seen as the paradigm shift to voting along lines of culture and values-divergences, when the Tory party emerged as the more viable option for those with Somewhere concerns. There are, however, certain weaknesses with the *Road to Somewhere* and these weaknesses mirror those of Haidt. In the first place, the overarching aim of Goodhart is to establish the legitimacy of Somewhere concerns, of belonging as an unavoidable necessity, which people cannot dismiss entirely. Holding to mere legitimacy as the primary aim, however, means he does not quite manage to articulate the 'combination' of Anywheres and Somewheres he seeks, but arrives at more of an uneasy ceasefire. Co-existence is not shared belonging. A 'less headstrong Anywhere liberalism' could accept that belonging can be legitimate and even subscribe to some measured form of belonging for itself. But can the legitimate ever inspire loyalty? It seems unlikely that people might make the move from accepting belonging as necessary to evincing loyalty towards that to which we belong.

As with Haidt, then, loyalty remains stubbornly awkward. To hold loyalty dear, to say it is important to cherish your belonging even when it goes against your values, points to an unconditional sense of attachment. For Haidt, attachment should be conditional on the good conduct of one's people, on being able to dial down belonging when the universal metrics of avoiding harm dictate. For Goodhart, belonging is conditional on a metric of efficacy. Anywheres are asked to accept that – '*successful* societies' are based on 'habits of coopera-tion, familiarity, trust and on bonds of language, history and culture' [my italics].[26] That is, belonging is conditional on success. This is not so much belonging to a particular place and particular people who live in that place, it is belonging as a generic concept that can foster a society's success. As with legitimacy, generic concepts do not inspire loyalty.

Loyalty is also problematic in light of the artificiality of Goodhart's practical proposals. He recommends that Anywheres ask themselves 'whether some minimal myths of common ancestry' may 'be neces-sary'.[27] He calls for people to embark on 'creating myths of common interest and identity'. Can created stories, carefully calibrated to invoke some esteem from those suspicious of belonging, really func-tion like a tacit set of shared assumptions? What happens to our exist-ing histories, stories and sagas, which served this purpose for English identity for centuries? The danger here comes by 'creating myths' and 'fashioning identities', not accepting Wendell Berry's maxim that 'neighbourhood is a given condition, not a contrived one'.[28] True loyalty is never contrived, for when loyalty is calculated, we are back to a loyalty which is apportioned only to that we deem worthy 'and not an iota more'.

Both Haidt and Goodhart offer some resources for easing the uneasy standoff between warring factions in a culture or society. But there is still a standoff. It is still a bit like being told that loyalty is 'the right thing to do', while it is tacitly accepted it is better to walk away and be free. Accommodating, tolerating, accepting the 'rightness' of loyalty in the name of co-existence is a far cry indeed from that 'deep social and cultural homogeneity' that engenders 'a spirit of reciprocity and belonging'.[29] What is called for is something more fundamental than reasoned argument in favour of belonging. Such arguments will always stand or fall on the conditions or premises by which belonging is defended against claims of illegitimacy. At Greenham, the unconditional attachment of child-bearing led directly into broader attachments to others. Something unconditional needs to pertain to one's cultural attachments, something primordial and visceral, something ultimately fostering an ongoing loyalty not dependent on some quantifiable metric.

On this front, Christopher Lasch offers some important insights. In *Culture of Narcissism*, Lasch maintains that contemporary culture evinces narcissistic character traits. Examples include 'dependence on the vicarious warmth provided by others combined with a fear of dependence', with 'a sense of inner emptiness, boundless unexpressed rage and unsatisfied oral cravings'.[30] It is not difficult to see why many hold that Lasch had prophetic insight, writing this in the late 1970s. 'Dependence on the vicarious warmth of others' could not be more prescient for the era of social media. A 'fear of dependence' is surely seen in the tendency to present people as what Lasch describes elsewhere as 'rootless abstractions wholly absorbed in maximizing their own advantage'.[31] Inward emptiness is well-attested by the ongoing pandemic around mental health and rage has exploded onto the streets during the 'wokesplosian' of summer 2020. 'Oral cravings' are surely indicated by a society with a deeply unhealthy relationship with food, particularly sugar, not to mention prescription drugs.

Drawing on Freud, Lasch holds that in very early infanthood the pain of separation from the mother and rage at having unmet biological needs endures pathologically in the narcissistic personality. Such a person seeks to 'annul the pain of disappointed love' by a slavish dependence on others for validation and an incessant attempt to fulfil needs rooted in infant experience.[32] The healthy personality, by contrast, learns to accept the inevitable separation from the mother and accepts that not all needs can be met on its terms. This involves a period of 'reparation' with the mother, accepting her human limitations, moving to a place of wisdom by acknowledging 'the union of gratification and suffering in a common source' and learning to accept its own 'dependence and limitations' in the process.[33] Those for whom this pathology becomes acute, however, are those who never undergo this reparative process via maturation. They are then fixated by trying to recreate the '"oceanic" contentment of the womb', the perpetual bliss with no separation or need.[34]

In contrast to Haidt and Goodhart, Lasch thus presents belonging as primordial rather than primitive. It is not something some people have progressed beyond, as such, but something that can provide generative orientation for life in stable people and cultures. It is not merely 'legitimate' to work through the visceral allegiance of early infanthood and into maturity, it is an undeniably positive and cele-bratory thing. We can extend Lasch's analysis to revisit the question of loyalty. A healthy personality accepts the mother's limitations, it does not make impossible demands on her and then throw itself into destructively trying to satisfy those demands elsewhere. This is a healthy acceptance of limit. Healthily accepting limits is the truer and the deeper loyalty; true loyalty is born of and continuous with the unconditional attachment of an infant towards its mother.

The German philosopher Peter Sloterdijk, like Lasch, draws con-nections between natality and culture. He challenges those who apply Freud's work to use the word 'transference' as 'a neurotic mecha-nism'.[35] Transference is the seeking of fulfilment of unmet needs from infancy onto other people and things. While this certainly often includes pathological behaviour, Sloterdijk maintains that some form of transference is a central aspect of human culture-formation. Transference is the 'gradual establishment' of an 'external womb' in which there is an ongoing symbiosis between people in a given local-ity.[36] This symbiosis, this sphere of reciprocity and belonging, is thus intrinsically rooted in the origins of each human life in the womb. Moreover, culture brings freedom to communities, a freedom from the vulnerability of individualism, from isolation, from fractiousness and the perpetual battle for resources. As he states, transference is 'the formal source of the creative process of the exodus of humans into the open', that is, into the fullness of life, biological and cultural.[37]

Transferring the loyalty of a child to its parent onto culture does not mean uncritically celebrating every episode in a nation's or culture's history. There is a Scylla and Charybdis of national loyalty: uncritical jingoism on the one hand, national self-loathing on the other. G. K. Chesterton points out that 'if a decent man's mother took to drink he would share her troubles to the last; but to talk as if he would be in a state of gay indifference as to whether his mother took to drink or not is certainly not the language of men who know the great mystery'.[38]

Loyalty is itself mysterious. The dedication humans can evince for each other can defy explanation. Rediscovering the virtuousness of this dedication will enable a sublime aspect of our humanity to return. It is sublime in the strict sense of this term, which describes things in art or nature that are not beautiful to look at but which are compelling, which stimulate awe and which enable us to glimpse that which is beyond our reckoning. In loyalty, people dedicate themselves to things neither beautiful nor even pleasing. The obedience of loyalty unleashes people from the captivity of esteeming only what they want to like. The result is a freedom to hold dear to that which it is difficult to love.

There was no one to invite to my mother's funeral. Within a few years of not answering letters and phone calls, she had lost contact with everyone she knew. So I asked people I knew to come instead, giving her the dignity of a decent send off. A few people commented to me afterwards that the last decades of her life would have been dreadful had I not been there during her decline. I ask myself now if perhaps the two disconnected strands of advice I got then seemed to have edged closer together at last. This was the fruit of the freedom that came through being loyal and which could never come were loyalty avoided.

3

Deference

In a squatted building on a Saturday night the party is going full throttle in the early hours of the morning. The room is pitch black, with fluorescent backdrops and UV lamps hanging on the walls. A strobe fires off flashes of light, dispensing steady streams of staccato snapshots of the scene. The snapshots come out in quick succession, then hang in the air around the dancefloor. Lingering like burns on scorched retinas, they leave ghostly silhouettes, which only gradually melt away. There is loss of balance in this sensory onslaught. People find their way in and out of the room by holding their arms out in front of them like zombies and moving alongside walls until they find a door, or holding onto more steady-footed associates who are guiding them. People stumble and lose their footing, they fall onto walls and ricochet back towards the ground, or knock over the speakers. Sometimes they grab the nearest person's leg on the way down and bring them to the ground too. If a number of people do this one after the other, there is a domino effect as each tumbles to the floor in turn. Some, however, have adjusted their eyes and ears to the chaos. They remain poised and focused, while confidently making their way around the room.

The venue was known locally as the Old Dole House. It was squatted for a few years in the mid 1990s, when these parties happened regularly. The cooperative that formed around the occupation included many circus-style performers. Fire-eaters went up-and-down the queues outside the building as people arrived and later gathered below the old disused railway arches out the back, as the crowd spilled out to watch the sunrise. Jugglers wandered around the rooms inside the building.

Above the main dancefloor a tightrope had been erected. A woman would mount the wire once the frenzy below had reached sufficient

intensity. Above the cacophony, she would steady herself before com-
mencing her walk. Her centre of gravity was firmly held within her
direct control. She would steadily make her way from one end of the
wire to the other, using a long balancing pole for assistance. On the
dancefloor below, people lost themselves in imbalance and confusion.
Above was a scene of self-possessed balance. The crowd cheered her
on and the woman would feed off the cheers, adopting riskier and
more daring displays of agility: hopping from one foot to another,
pirouetting, genuflecting on one knee and holding her balancing pole
vertically up high into the air above her, while slowly lowering her
head in a bow.

The Old Dole House had previously been a benefits office where
people signed on every fortnight to receive their welfare payments.
The cooperative pointed to a continuity between this former use and
its more recent requisition. At the tail-end of Thatcherism, a symbol
of a once-strong public sector was again in common use. It was oft-
repeated that the then prime minister, John Major, had signed on here
before he became a civil servant. This legend is topsy-turvy; the future
prime minister of Great Britain in a social security office in grotty
Brixton. Like with the tightrope-walking woman, people fed off the
thought of this contradictory spectacle, endlessly repeating the story
about a man at the top rubbing shoulders with those at the bottom.
People from high echelons of society brushed up against the lowest at
the parties too. There were far more privately educated trustafarians
among the organizers than they cared to admit, along with many
down-at-heel characters too. Members of the criminal underclass clustered around staircases and the empty side-rooms where drugs were
sold and exchanged. They were adept at pickpocketing or mugging
unwary revellers who had travelled to Brixton from their homes in
Hampstead and Highgate, or piled into taxis to keep partying after
the bars shut in central London.

The cooperative was evicted in 1995. The building was reoccupied
by different groups on a couple of occasions afterwards and then,
after roofs collapsed, it lay derelict for a while. The criminal element
of the first parties had their day in the year 2000. A group of south
London reprobates brought their sound system and set it up at the

back of the building's rotting remains, under the railway arches where people used to gather at dawn. The timber beams of the decrepit municipal building now rose like the decaying ribcage of a huge carcass on either side of the dancefloor. The psychedelic imagery of the earlier parties had disappeared, the circus performers were gone. The mood was dark and aggressive. The party went on all weekend and there were numerous brawls and fistfights. Assailants would tear across the dancefloor, dragging partygoers this way and that as kicks and punches flew. The levels of intoxication were so extreme hardly anyone seemed able to walk or stand unaided. A group had found an old staircase in the building's remains and scrambled up to the last section of roof still standing. They stood high above the scene, staggering about and shouting at the people below.

The Old Dole House was knocked down in 2007 and the site was wasteland before luxury apartments were built there in a development named Brixton Square. The brochure for these properties is clearly written for people who do not know London at all, nor even the country of which it is the capital. Those who remember the parties complain that this private requisition of the land is a betrayal of their memories. This was where the future prime minister queued alongside unemployed tradesmen; here dropout aristocrats and local hooligans were thrown together during the 1990s. Now it is a sequestered haven for the rich, with no intermingling between social classes. Salt was rubbed in the wound when the marketing for the plush new flats used a typeface that aped the 1990s techno-punk aesthetic. The old hierarchies had been restored by the evils of capital, they said. Brixton Square was like a Victorian factory-owner's house, where the wealthy were protected from the sights and smells of the grimy peasants who worked his machines.

The local folk traditions about the Old Dole House are beloved by those who are haters of hierarchy. They say they saw glimpses of a flattened-out social order and that was disfigured again by the deluxe apartments. But, if the retelling of these memories is driven by the hatred of hierarchy, a different interpretation comes to light. The developers of the flats, Barrett Homes, have an inclusion statement reassuring people that 'We value everyone for who they are and the unique contribution they bring' and 'we actively ensure our opportunities are available to the widest possible pool of people to reflect our diverse society'. This is not something a Victorian factory-owner would have said. The incomers to a newly gentrified borough are hardly repelled by the area's grimy past, as earlier beneficiaries of capitalism were disgusted by putrid slum dwellings. Rather, they are attracted by the kudos that comes with living somewhere regarded in the popular mind as a notorious ghetto. The dubious history is sanitized, re-presented and celebrated for the incomers' consumption, like the urban music reviewed in Saturday's *Guardian*.

The same applies to the area's political pasts. Vicinities like this had what were grandly called the 'head offices' of all manner of 'People's Front of Judea'-type revolutionary groups or cooperatives in tatty rooms with typewriters over high-street shops. Now, the radical activities are repackaged as selling points. Pop-up exhibitions of photography archives from those days allow wealthy white thirty-somethings to bask in their alternative credentials, while enjoying soy lattes and gluten-free pastries. Coffee-table books of remastered polaroids of the old cooperatives are found in their apartments, filled with images of protests against racist policing, in support of the miners or the women of Greenham, and images of reggae bands playing at benefit gigs in Brockwell Park. Even the wardrobes of the interlopers are tinged with a faux-radical aesthetic; they wear donkey jackets like the binmen during the Winter of Discontent and the 1980s tracksuits and Adidas trainers the local youths once wore to copy their counterparts in Harlem or the Bronx. Thankfully, today's polite norms around cultural appropriation mean these white trustafarians no longer have dreadlocks and string vests in the colours of the Jamaican flag. Just as it was then, however, these people continue to cultivate their identity around the area's history, while never associating with the locals themselves.

It is therefore incorrect to speak of a rupture in the history of the land on which the Old Dole House stood. The new residents are haters of hierarchy too. They would nod in approval at valuing 'everyone for who they are and the unique contribution they bring'. In some ways Brixton Square actually epitomizes the recent history of the place. For the hatred of hierarchy ever gives way to crueler and more insidious pecking orders, to social structures more stratified than those once rebuked. Like the new residents, the old squatters would nod in approval with the inclusion statement of the developers, if they didn't know who wrote it. A flyer for one of the first parties described the dress code by saying: 'Be yourself, who else are you going to be?' A crazy character like the tightrope-walking woman was valued with rapturous cheers 'for the unique contribution' she brought to the proceedings.

Yet beneath her the unruly rabble staggered about. They watched in admiration someone who could play the dynamics of the scene to her advantage, someone who could display balance and poise amid all the precarity and instability. She held her centre of gravity within herself. The incomers to the area, who play today's dynamics to their advantage, are similarly perceptible for their self-possession. Locals frequently comment on their conceited air. These are people skilled at presenting themselves as well-placed in feeling valued 'for who they are and the unique contribution they bring'.

For all the hatred of hierarchy espoused back then, the unruly rabble below the tightrope walker actually were themselves genuinely reminiscent of the Victorian era. The ghostly silhouettes of London's Victorian past lingered about them. Encountering them felt like wandering into a scene from Dickens. There were little urchins lifting whatever they could from people's pockets, a brutish Bill Sikes-type old punk rowing with a tarty companion and with a scraggy hound running alongside his feet. Instead of gathering around morsels of bread or gruel, the new urchins clustered around sedatives and stimulants. In the candlelit area hidden away behind the DJ booth, long-haired Fagin-type ancient hippies lurked, who had long since found ways to ensure an income from the subterranean economy. This was an *Oliver Twist* where the flatcaps were baseball caps, the hobnail boots battered Air Max, the silk handkerchiefs being pilfered then were now Ray-Ban shades. The prize of all prizes was a credit card with an easily forgeable signature, rather than the old five-bob note.

Many of the middle-class kids at the parties saw this world up close for the only time in their lives. Their boomer upbringings and trendy north London educations meant they looked upon the underworld's inhabitants with great esteem. They would even copy the dress and manners of speech of those who would barge them out of the way, those who would sometimes threaten and rob them. Hatred of hierarchy entails a refusal to accept one's position in society, followed by attempts to pretend you belong elsewhere. Here the impression of being in a novel by Dickens breaks down. There are no gentlemen there who seek to emulate the lower orders. The noble Mr Brownlow, who takes Oliver in, would never dress like Bill Sikes or try to adopt his accent. Nor would Fagin try to pass as someone of Mr Brownlow's station, nor Nancy masquerade as a lady from polite society.

Dickens was no hater of hierarchy. He offers some of the most disturbing descriptions of an appallingly unequal society, yet writes with a profound even-handedness towards both rich and poor. When Nancy is reluctant to comply with Fagin's plan to recapture Oliver from the police station after his arrest, he comments on her 'polite and delicate evasion of the request', which showed a 'natural good breeding which cannot bear to inflict upon a fellow-creature the pain of a direct and painful refusal'.[1] He set out to write about the 'dregs of life' in 'all their wretchedness'. Yet he shocked his readers by dwelling on how members of the underclass were often guilty of pride, something then associated only with those at the top. He calls pride 'the vice of the lowest and most debased creatures no less than of the high and self-assured'.[2]

Vices are also on plentiful display among the well-to-do who run the orphanages and workhouses; those 'held in high respect and admiration', he says, have 'a decided propensity for bullying' and derive 'no inconceivable pleasure from the exercise of petty cruelty'.[3] As put by Gertrud Himmelfarb, 'the "good" individuals do not correspond with the poor, nor the "bad" with the rich', for '[v]irtues and vices are equally distributed among all classes'.[4] G. K. Chesterton claims that Dickens was 'the living expression of the French Revolution's philosophy of equality and liberty'.[5] This mocked the intellectuals of Chesterton's day, who thought themselves the epitome of high revolutionary ideals but were completely unable to relate to those they sought to save from their misery. Having spent his boyhood with 'the masses of London', says Chesterton, Dickens 'hated nothing more than the patronizing attitude of intellectuals towards them'.[6]

Dickens combines an acceptance of hierarchy with a critique of society's ills and injustices. This is because his corrective impulses are not ideological, but moral. As George Orwell notes, '[i]t would be difficult to point anywhere in his books to a passage suggesting that the economic system is wrong *as a system*'. There 'is no clear sign that he wants the existing order to be overthrown or that he believes it would make much difference if it *were* overthrown', for 'his target is not so much society as "human nature"'.[7]

It is rare for Chesterton and Orwell to agree on something, but each notice a medievalism to Dickens' work. While the novelist himself loathed the fashionable medievalism of the nineteenth-century intellectuals, Chesterton points out that Dickens' writing is actually the more medieval in sensibility. This is shown particularly by his descriptions of food, feasts and joviality, the endless drama of paupers and their masters. For Orwell, Dickens is medieval enough to be positively feudal, precisely due to his acceptance of hierarchy. When 'he wants to draw a sympathetic picture of a servant', he writes, 'he creates what is recognizably a feudal type'; people who 'identity themselves with their master's family' and are 'doggishly faithful'.[8] Of course, this still upsets those committed to an ideological system supposing such sentiments must never resurface.

There is another rare moment of concurrence between Chesterton and Orwell on Dickens. Both of them notice how middle-class ideologues tend to cultivate a superficial resemblance to the poor, while simultaneously being unable to interact with them. This is why Chesterton considered Dickens' writings a worthy antidote to the *fin de siècle* spirit of his time because those intellectuals and writers exhibited such 'contempt for the common man'.[9] For Orwell, the novelist is popular with ordinary people because '[t]he common man' still lives in Dickens' 'mental world', when 'nearly every modern intellectual' would write it off as 'bourgeois morality'. Dickens can thus portray the working classes with personal familiarity, yet 'he does not wish to resemble them'.[10] It is the haters of hierarchy who blend unfamiliarity with the people with trying to look and sound like them from afar.

There is an important exception to the rule of Dickens' characters not copying those of a different station in life: the Artful Dodger. He is a walking contradiction. He is deeply implicated alongside the most wretched characters, first bringing Oliver to Fagin's den, and forever acting in dutiful service to his rotten master in all manner of schemes and wiles. Orwell claims that Dickens wrote of the criminal poor with repulsion and saved his more admiring prose for 'the ordinary, decent, labouring poor'.[11] While such one-dimensional characterization is generally typical, there is much more than mere wretchedness to the Dodger. Perhaps a complexity of character is apportioned to him because he was taken in by a criminal gang at an age young enough to ambiguate his moral culpability. This complexity is demonstrated by his topsy-turvy appearance. He is at once both young and old, rich and poor: 'as dirty a juvenile as one would wish to see' but having 'all the airs and manners of a man'. He dresses clumsily in the garments of a city gent, with a smart but dirty hat and coat many sizes too big, presenting himself 'as roystering and swaggering a young gentleman as ever stood four feet six'.[12]

The Dodger's emulation of the richer class reaches an apogee in the courtroom scene, which ends with his being sent to the penal colonies on a life sentence. The contradictoriness of his character dominates the account. His arrest was for being in possession of a stolen snuff box, a mere trifle for one who had pilfered the rich of so many expensive goods for years. Prior to the Dodger's case being heard, Fagin decries his arrest for such a petty theft as a great dishonour to a criminal scamp of such renown: 'Oh, why didn't he rob some rich old gentleman . . . and go out as a gentleman and not like a common prig, without no honour nor glory!'[13] But Fagin then imagines him in court, dazzling the judge with his cockney eloquence and confident demeanour. This is what happens when the Dodger tells the magistrate that his attorney is taking breakfast at the House of Commons that morning and that his 'respectable circle of acquaintance' will react with fury when they find out he is in the dock. There is great amusement at the topsy-turvy legend, the street-kid claiming to rub shoulders with people at Westminster, the inversion of John Major signing-on in Brixton.

Nonetheless, the Dodger's absurd clothing does nothing to disguise the reality of his situation. He does not dress this way to try to pass as a city gent, but to signify his proficiency as a criminal street-kid to his peers. There is an analogy here with the wealthy inhabitants of gentrified London trying to dress like the original residents. There is always a retro tinge, an ironic twist. They never dress like today's poor, but like those at a safe distance of twenty or thirty years ago. It is a sign of tasteful bourgeois status, not proletarian belonging. A disguise, by contrast, genuinely conceals the true identity of a person. For Dickens' characters, true identities are disguised by stations in life, always separate from wealth and status. That is, everyone, at their core, has equality of opportunity in the moral sense, the same number of occasions to cultivate either virtue or vice. Similarly, the society he portrays will always have a variance in the moral equality of outcome, whatever system is in place.

Saints and sinners will ever lurk among the highest and the lowest and ever be found distributed in due proportion among the layers in between. Haters of hierarchy don't wear disguises, they adopt superficial resemblances to signal that they are playing the dynamics of the social order fluently, while conceitedly pretending to rebuke that order in the name of radicalism. Like the tightrope-walking woman, they adopt a performative posture of obeisance, a mocking bow. Yet the rightful acceptance of hierarchy does involve a measure of disguise. This is not disguise in the sense of deception, but in the sense of having discretion. The rightful acceptance of hierarchy entails holding back the moral worth of each person, apart from the socio-economic role they have to play in the greater scheme of things. The full acceptance of the role apportioned to oneself requires understanding that that role neither reflects nor exhausts one's moral worth.

In the Victorian era, a word was current among the London poor, which has since developed new and inauthentic meanings but which has an unwritten lineage disclosing something of an old lore. This lore mandates that each person's moral worth must not be confused with their appointed role in society. This lore is not just antithetical to today's world, but repulsive to it. Its statutes maintain that, by and large, it is good for people to accept their station in life and not be driven by the urge to acquire greater wealth and status. It holds that there is 'social virtue in staying put'.[14] This is not to say there cannot be naturally occurring exchanges this way and that, as circumstance requires. Nor is it a mere acceptance of the injustices that ever attend economic inequality. Rather, it supposes that the hatred of hierarchies causes more injustice than it does justice so, rather than do away with them, the task is to make them function more justly. To obey this lore is to untangle moral worth from economic worth; accepting the truth of the former is always concealed from, and must not be confused with, the latter.

This old lore of discretion can be found by focusing attention on the old word 'geezer'. Geezer has suffered considerable slippage in its proper meanings. It is often used simply for 'working-class male' or 'cockney' or, sometimes, a wideboy or even someone like the Artful Dodger. This slippage is itself illustrative, in that it arises from the fact that, properly used, the word appears not to mean anything particularly at all, like the word 'bloke'. Yet it doesn't really mean bloke, it is close to 'a good bloke', but carries a sense of artfulness with it, an artfulness not in any way dodgy. It derives from the word disguise, as in a disguiser, then a -guiser, eventually becoming geezer.

It is rare to encounter the authentic use of the term today. It used to be heard every night in the public house, but there are fewer pubs now and those that remain rarely have the place they once did in people's lives. You can still hear it spoken in unremarkable barber shops and among the cab drivers who bear its legacy about town. Sometimes it is heard in those cafés where continuity with the past is unbroken. It was once heard particularly among those who sold the *Evening Standard* outside the Tube stations in the late afternoon and early evening, before that paper became a freesheet. Then the old newspaper sellers refused to take hourly paid positions to dish out their wares freely and they were gone.

By today's standards the geezer is a locus of contradictions, whereas in truth he is the site where opposites interplay. His manner is always unfeigned, because he happily plays a role. He is self-assured, because he is humble. He is never obsequious, because he accepts his place in life without regret. He is respectful to others, but only because he understands they are playing a role. He is genuinely personable, because he maintains distance from people. He is never showy or ostentatious, because he dresses well. He is never insanely drunk, because he enjoys a drink. He is generally found in the company of men, because he respects women greatly. He knows when people are taking liberties, because he likes to pay for others. He is never lost in agonized introspection, because he is naturally reflective. He treats his earnings as if they were gifts, because he works hard and doesn't feel entitled.

The geezer embodies another word rarely heard today: equanimity. Equanimity is different from self-possession. The geezer doesn't possess himself because he is not the measure of all things. The equanimous one has a fairness or evenness of soul (*anima*) because his centre of gravity is borne outside of himself. His perspective is broad and deep; he knows he is but one small element of a much greater whole. The self-possessed one, by contrast, holds his centre of gravity firmly within his direct control. He signals to the world how adept he is at playing the dynamics of the system to his advantage, then comes tumbling down when things don't go his way. The spectacle of the tightrope walker shows self-possession, but the balance of the geezer shows equanimity.

The lore of the geezer dictates that stations in life do not disclose a person's value, hence its root meaning of 'disguise'. To confuse these two is to shift the centre of gravity into oneself. Then socio-economic esteem becomes an exhaustive signifier of personal value. Playing a role considered menial or low-status is then failure, climbing up the greasy pole a sign of personal impressiveness. Holding them apart means one's centre of gravity resides in systems bigger than oneself. Life is then much less focused on one's own earnings and status and on the wellbeing of the whole of the systems to which one contributes. Equanimity necessitates participation in networks of kinship, social associations, societal structuring and cultural identity. These give a genuine stability to one's sense of self, far preferable to the acquisition of wealth and status.

Disentangling moral from economic value enables people to cherish their callings in life, not always to chase after things perceived as bigger and better. This separation shows itself in the willingness to defer. To defer to someone in another station is to accept that their experience and judgement of the matter is superior to yours. It must be stated immediately that deference is not a concept to be applied in one, 'upward', direction, although it is commonly mistaken as such today. This mistake says more about our society than it does about the word itself. People defer to those with experiences and judgements more applicable to the case at hand than themselves. If moral and economic value are confused, deference is mistaken for obsequiousness to those in a more powerful position, a sickeningly servile devotion. But the word only means an obedient acceptance of another's vantage point as better than one's own. Anyone who calls a plumber to fix his boiler is being deferent.

Confusing moral and economic leads to a hatred of hierarchy as something intrinsically wrong. Then hatred of hierarchy causes ever-more stratified structures to be set up instead, because everyone is scrabbling to get to the top. Deference to those deemed 'higher' is acutely painful, because you feel as if you're accepting that they are better than yourself. Deference to those deemed 'lower' is impossible and everything is reduced to the material element of any exchange. Then a professional is not deferring to a plumber fixing the boiler, he's paying someone else to do it because he thinks he has better things to do. In a scrabble to the top, it requires ever greater feats of panache to get there; those who have made it seem a million miles away from those who have not. As Wendell Berry says, 'our society is at once "highly stratified and highly mobile"'.[15] Social mobility might be taken by most as some wonderful freedom, but in truth it indicates a system that restrains people from flourishing as they are. Obedience to one's situation grants the more genuine freedom, the freedom of equanimity, the levity that comes with having evenness of soul.

A properly functioning hierarchy doesn't need to make a big thing of mobility, because there is a genuine exchange and interaction

between the different levels in that people defer. In a properly functioning hierarchy people do not need to imitate those situated on
a different rung of the ladder, because one can defer to them. This
is because there is exchange and interaction between people who
understand they depend on others to perform the duties proper to
their station. The exchange is not between lives deemed successful or
unsuccessful. Each participant bears responsibility in some sense for
the other through the work they undertake. Mobility prohibits interrelationship, which needs the differentiation of deference to function.
You don't need to travel to somewhere that is present among you by
what it provides. The *oblige* of *noblesse oblige* is the forgotten side of
a broken binary, now mistaken only for what Orwell called 'doggish
faithfulness' on the other.

The scrabble to the top leaves people wanting to emulate something like the tightrope walker, who can balance among the precarity
to great effect. But it generates far more people like the unruly rabble
below, stumbling about in the precarity and imbalance, unable to find
their poise. There are also far more original residents of the gentrified
areas than the new incomers, but they recede into the background,
unnoticed, as the new residents strut about town in desirable clothes
to attend alluring eateries. Haters of hierarchy recognize this fact and
so erect safety nets for those falling to the bottom. The benefits system
is already indicative of a society that has ceased to function properly,
which has failed to provide the means by which people can live. Yes,
it is better to have provision for people in need rather than let them
suffer in poverty, but – however well-intentioned – this can become
a further means of stratification for people then seen as objects of
pity. People don't defer to those on benefits, because society does not
enable them to contribute to the greater whole.

Those who see others 'up sticks' and make their way to the top while
they are left behind can be left despondent in their sense of self.
Those of dubious socio-economic value are led to consider their lives
almost worthless. A society that finds deference distasteful replaces
it with apparently more amenable and pleasing concepts. The way to
make this system more palatable is to write around it a narrative of

affliction. Faced with the undigestible blend of moral and economic worth in practical reality, people present a contradictory narrative of affliction so as to protect themselves from the dark reality. That is, not climbing up the ladder of wealth and status is presented as an unfair consequence of some undeserved circumstance, be it ill-health, systematic oppression, a disfunctional upbringing or addiction. But these narratives of affliction just mask the conceptual confusion of moral and socio-economic worth that allows those at the top never to defer to those on whom they should depend for the smooth running of the whole. Affliction provides a way to pretend that, as personal value and social status are at odds for so many, this is not because they are fundamentally different in themselves, but rather because some external circumstance has made it so. Affliction is thus imitative, it imitates the separation of moral and economic worth, rather than holds each as disguised in the other.

Dickens considered hierarchies as natural facts of life. A philosopher who has written on narratives of affliction, Mark Fisher, argues that now mental ill-health is considered as 'a natural fact'.[16] Overwhelming feelings of despondency and worthlessness attend those slipping downward; anxiety and panic afflict those struggling to maintain balance somewhere higher up. So people are encouraged to understand their neurological chemistry as topsy-turvy, thus explaining their dis-ease with their place within the system. Drawing on his experience as lecturing in further education, Fisher says that 'being a teenager in late capitalist Britain is now close to being reclassified as a sickness' because mental disorders are so endemic among adolescents.[17] He claims an antidote can be found with a 'politicization' of 'common disorders' like depression and stress, so the 'social system' of capitalism is then rightly understood as 'inherently dysfunctional'.[18] Otherwise, a poor quality of life is simply written off as 'chemical imbalances in the individual's neurology and/or by family background'.[19]

Fisher mentions Slavoj Žižek's observation that today's world esteems 'being smart'. This 'smartness' is analogous to the poise of the tightrope walker, of a world where 'spontaneous interaction and autopoiesis' take precedence 'against fixed hierarchy'.[20] Fisher also draws on Richard Sennet's observation that today's 'conditions of permanent instability' have such deleterious effects because the place of 'respite from the pressures of the world', namely the family, requires for its functioning the very values today's 'smart' world assumes obsolete: 'obligation, trustworthiness, commitment'.[21] What he calls the 'chemico-biologization of mental illness' steps in to heal the wounds, but then perpetuates them, reinforcing capitalism's 'drive to atomistic individualism' by situating the problem in one's brain, while bringing great dividends to the pharmaceutical industry.[22]

Fisher is on shakier ground, however, when he agrees with Alain Badiou and David Henry that the stratifications brought by the globalized neoliberal order are a 'Restoration', a '*return* of class power and privilege'.[23] When were class power and privilege not present; when was it so egalitarian that there could be a marked return? Badiou adopts the term Restoration from the return of the French monarchy in 1815, but surely return was able to happen, at least in part, because the revolutionary haters of hierarchy had erected a more unjust system in place of the old. Moreover, since Fisher wrote his analysis, there are other elements at play. The flattening out of disparities in material privilege has now been deprioritized by the newer narratives of affliction provided by identity politics. Material privilege is no longer seen as the primary site of injustice. We are now expected to include the wealthy among the oppressed and ignore economic reality altogether. Now even a royal prince presents himself as a victim of systemic oppression. Even if a state of 'fully automated luxury communism' were achieved, prescriptions for serotonin reuptake inhibitors would surely be required to soften the impact of microaggressive slights towards whatever identarian characteristic is in vogue at any given time.

Lasch's *Culture of Narcissism* provides a contrast to Fisher's approach. Taking issue with meritocracy, Lasch makes points from across the Atlantic, which resonate with the old lore of the geezer. He notes that 'success has never been so closely associated with mobility' and sees this as a misappropriation of 'the democratic ideal', which was once about 'a rough equality of condition' but is now taken to mean 'the selective promotion of elites into the professional-managerial class'.[24] He also gets to the nub of the differences between the old gentlemanly elite and those who are 'being smart', saying an 'aristocracy of talent' prohibits the *'noblesse oblige'* which meant 'a willingness to make a direct and personal contribution to the public good'.[25] But, while Fisher notes that mental ill-health softens the edges of the new system, for Lasch it is a therapeutic, not pharmaceutical, paradigm. He calls this the 'democratization of "self-esteem"'. People are told to 'esteem' themselves greatly; this is shown particularly by the 'recovery movement', which seeks 'to counter the oppressive sense of failure in those who fail to climb the educational ladder'.[26] He says 'meritocracy generates an obsessive concern with self-esteem' and he points out that the phrase 'dignity of labour' lost currency at exactly the time 'social mobility' entered 'the academic vocabulary'.[27]

For Lasch, the dominant therapeutic paradigm fosters an artificial 'empathy' and 'understanding' for others, which is manufactured 'without risk'. This instils a profound inequality, 'under the pretence that everyone is special in their own way'.[28] We thus find ourselves back with the inclusion of statements of the developers of Brixton Square, 'valuing everyone for the unique contribution they bring' and with the dress code of the parties at the old Dole House: 'Be yourself, who else who are you going to be?' For the rabble caught up in the fray below the tightrope walker, there is little hope for equanimity, little chance of holding their centre of gravity outside themselves. This is because the system is now, as Fisher notes, 'centreless'. There is no centre to global capitalism; it is too big, too vast. It processes formulae of unfathomable complexity through technocratic codes of which only the 'smartest' players are aware. As long as the centre is missing, there is no sense of a greater whole where individual contributions can be considered meaningful. A system without a centre ceases to be a system and becomes an infinitely pervasive force. It is impossible to defer when under the influence of the 'shadowy, centreless personality' of global capital.[29] The haters of hierarchy are thus left to imitate deference through imposing narratives of affliction, with all the sincerity of the tightrope walker in the old Dole House when she took the knee and slowly lowered her head in a bow.

4

Honour

Fritjof Capra's *The Tao of Physics* (1974) describes an experience the author had while sitting by the ocean on a summer's afternoon. He 'suddenly became aware of [his] whole environment as being engaged in a gigantic cosmic dance'. As a physicist, he says: 'I knew the sand, rocks, water and air around me were made of vibrating molecules and atoms and that these consisted of particles which interacted with one another by creating and destroying other particles.' He also knew 'the Earth's atmosphere was continually bombarded by showers of "cosmic rays", particles of high energy undergoing multiple collisions as they penetrated the air'. His training in physics coalesced with his interest in Eastern Mysticism: 'I "saw" the atoms of the elements and those of my body participating in this cosmic dance of energy . . . at the moment I *knew* that this was the Dance of Shiva.'[1]

Capra is a child of the 1960s. He considers that decade as ground zero for a new aeon of peace and love. He places great faith in the authority of natural science and is dedicated to ecology. He celebrates the sacred traditions of the East. Science and mysticism enable him to see the inner reality of the world and know its truth intimately. He says the vision by the oceanside was provoked at least in part by his previous consumption of 'power plants', meaning psychedelic substances.

Many now experiment with mind-altering drugs in their youth and forget the experiences as they mature. But some remain haunted by the things they have seen. Others, like Capra, cherish their memories as holding deep significance. Whether the memories are intrusive or welcome, they linger in permanently altered minds, like burns on scorched retinas leave ghostly silhouettes, colouring everything else in sight. Since the 1960s, large numbers of people in Western societies have ingested mind-altering drugs. The alteration of human consciousness surely registers in the character of Western cultures. Maybe those cultures themselves have been permanently altered too. Then everyone's cultural retinas are burned, we see all the world in a blurred and malformed way, because our means of understanding – that is, culture – has been indelibly scarred. Either way, Capra certainly shares many interests of Western citizens today. The prevalence of self-help cults, cod-spirituality, popular science and Boomeresque politics suggests the new aeon he heralded is indeed well underway.

Capra mentions the effect of seeing the first photovisual images of planet Earth after the moon landings of 1969. He claims this was hugely important for enabling a global consciousness to emerge, now people could see the oneness of their planet visually, Earth as a cohesive unit. There are similarities with his vision of the Dance of Shiva. A member of the select elite attains a heavenly vantage point and sees something profound, something not granted to mere mortals. This vantage point enables a vision of the 'totality', something mere mortals cannot see from the limited perspective of their tiny portion of it. This totality then transmits some spiritual gnosis which causes the Woodstock generation's view of the world to take shape.

However, this viewing of the world seems rather just to endorse the way the world was already being viewed by this generation anyway. Stewart Brand claimed before Capra that the first photo taken of the entire planet from the ATS-3 satellite in 1967 would alter the human mind in such a way that 'no one would ever perceive things the same way' again. But he had this idea during an acid trip a year previously, in 1966.[2] The *Boomerweltanschauung* was endorsed, not created. Seeing the world as globalized now had photographic form. The downgrading of day-to-day spheres of responsibility was just accelerated, now they were mere trifles belonging to a fragment of the great totality. They were born of a perspective so limited as to be illusory, even. This illusoriness is reminiscent of the *Samsara* of the East, the material world of death and rebirth from whence a visionary must escape to the ultimate reality beyond, where all of us are One.

The internet grew out of such Boomerism. It would be truly global, even transcendent, enabling us to rise above Samsara's laws of space and time. It would be truly democratic, its means of production not controlled by the bigoted old aristocracy. It would be a vehicle of free expression, with no censorship or control. On all fronts, however, the technology has inverted each of these intentions. Let us put ourselves in Capra's shoes and imagine how his vision of the Dance of Shiva might apply to the digital age. We can imagine all the unseen energies floating about us, transmitted by mobile phone aerials and transmitters, fibreoptic signals pulsating through channels in the earth beneath, the atmosphere bathed in electromagnetic ciphers gliding between gadgets and routers via wi-fi, everything permeated with dancing luminosity.

If the screens of electronic devices are taken to be tiny portions of the great unseen totality, then all about us swim instant messages of people relaying the minutiae of their day, information about current affairs are being commented on in 'real' time, not the illusory earthbound time of Samsara. Bleeps and signals flutter down from satellites encircling Earth and buzz around our ears, communicating with us via apps that enable people to navigate around town, to shop, read or play games. There are countless films being streamed, not to mention the vast cornucopia of diverse music. Infinitesimal rays of glowing light radiating informational cargo saturate our bodies.

Before long, however, our minds will turn to another element of this great totality. Like Big Tech censorship or the mining of minerals for smart phones, this element betrays the early phantasmagoria of proponents of the *Boomerweltanschauung*: pornography.

Helen Andrews writes, '[h]istorians of the twenty-fifth century with three paragraphs to give to the twenty-first in their textbooks will be more likely to mention the proliferation of pornography than any living president'. She goes on, '[i]t is impossible for people under thirty to understand how porn-saturated their world is compared with any other period in history'. Now '[a]ny thirteen-year-old with a smart-phone can watch video of almost any sex act he cares to, as often as he likes, for free and in total privacy'.[3] Replaying Capra's vision for the digital age means Shiva is joined by Rati, goddess of love, lust and pleasure. Rati's iconography often has vast numbers of naked women caught up limb-to-limb in strange postural contortions, images which would once have made people blush. The fact they now barely register as even mildly risqué reflects the permanently scorched vision with which we see them.

Yet even Rati doesn't capture the totality. To consider 'love, lust and pleasure' as exhaustive of the consequences of using the internet to satisfy sexual desire is woefully naive. Beyond every private moment of satisfaction gleaned from the tiny portion of the totality, the screen, there is the life of the people in the pornographic images. There is the desperation which led to such dehumanization, the demoralization that will haunt them with far more ferocity than any bad trip. This is not to mention more sinister elements: the women who have been trafficked, drugged up with anaesthetic and aphrodisiac variants of what Capra calls 'power plants' and physically intimidated into 'performing'. Then it gets even worse, considering many of those participating in the images are barely adults and a very great number of them are mere children, even babies. Capra saw the Earth's atmosphere continually bombarded by cosmic rays. Now it is bombarded with porn. He delighted at 'particles of high energy' penetrating the air. Now even the air about us is being penetrated without our consent.

These sinister facts cannot quite be captured by the ancient myths of Rati. The most merciless acts of the Hindu gods and goddesses are only ever meting out *Danda* or bad karma. Karma is a reassuring doctrine, a belief that somehow and somewhere all of those who cause suffering to others will get their just desserts. The traffickers will pay the price, we just need to behold the totality. Unspeakable cruelty only appears as such when a tiny portion is taken as the greater whole. Evil is ultimately illusory, because it is provisional. The evildoer will be forced to mend his ways. Viewing the totality thus brings satisfaction. The wounds accrued in this life will not leave scars, scorched skin will not have burns, because other lives lived elsewhere in the great totality will bring all things together. For we are all One.

Some Westerners once dismissed such myths as naive and childish, compared to the grave moral teachings of Christianity. Today, this dismissal is reversed. Christian moral teachings are seen as infantile, obsessively telling people when it is wrong to have sex.

Traditions of the East are seen as founts of metaphysical wisdom for those developed souls who have outgrown the need to be dogmatic and sanctimonious. In truth, neither are childish. It is ignorant to dismiss mythologies as just stories. Myths bespeak mysteries, they portray the profound. The images are a tiny portion of a totality, pointing symbolically to great forces of nature, of humanity, and of cosmic reality. In this way, science and myth are analogous, albeit in a way different to Capra's presentation. Both science and myth give visual and spoken form to unseen realities, each gives a language and a set of conceptual tools for the *truer* reality going on behind, beyond, above or within the world we behold in daily life. Be it the genomic sequencing of virus particles or a moon goddess drawing in the oceanic tides, both science and myth provide ways to explain why things are the way they are. Both discern and depict a realm of causation that explains the effects among which we live each day and night. Both seek to resolve the questions we face in earthly phenomena and to show how to manipulate those phenomena to our advantage.

Notwithstanding their often puerile nature, even urban myths and conspiracy theories function within these explanatory dynamics. When the coronavirus pandemic first broke in the UK, there was a spate of vandalism against mobile phone masts, because people thought the virus was caused by 5G data technology. Absurd as it is, we can still ask why it was *this*, specifically, that captured people's imaginations. It could bespeak an intuitive sense that our cultural atmosphere is increasingly permeated with things that are unsanitary and deleterious, that those in power are more culpable for this fact than they care to admit. Why is it that almost any thinkpiece on pornography will use the word 'saturation'; is it just about sheer volume or pointing to its ubiquity in the atmosphere? Modern-day myths, like those behind Pizzagate or QAnon, have child sexual abuse as the motivating factor behind their baddies. Again, such things may resonate because people sense that powerful people are in denial, sometimes even witting facilitation, of the sexual abuse of children going on in their midst. The cases of Jeffrey Epstein and Jimmy Savile continue to pour fuel on these flames. Fantastical narratives never emerge *ex nihilo*. They are made of the pre-existent matter floating around in the culture in which they come forth.

The *Boomerweltanshauung* promises the satisfaction of desire. There are two movements at play here, the first political, the second spiritual. In the first place, children were once told 'life isn't fair'. Now they are told, 'you can make of this world everything you want'. The first epithet restrains desire and limits its purchase, the second promises it satisfaction. The first honours reality, because it does not put the totality of reality within the child's grasp. It treats reality with respect, as something far greater than a means of attaining satisfaction. To claim everything is within your grasp is to dishonour reality. It foments utopianism. Everyone can then be satisfied, through all the world. This tendency was displayed by the optimism of the '68ers' and reaches a crescendo in people like Jeffrey Sachs or Bill Gates. The instinctive kickback against cruelty, greed and selfishness will finally find contentment and rest. A worldly nirvana awaits.

When this nirvana takes much longer than expected to be realized, the second movement occurs. The Boomer's yearning for satisfaction thirsts instead for spiritual contentment, for something like the original *Nirvana* of Eastern mysticism. The problem is then seen as desiring itself and contentment seen as coming from detachment. But, more often than not, the desire for satisfaction isn't really negated. The moment of satisfaction is just transferred to some higher plane. The will to make the world perfect projects a state of perfect satisfaction behind, beyond or above the world – somewhere in the heavenly ether.

To consider the satisfaction of desire as all-important engenders a fixation with totalities. To give an example of a contrasting approach, Aristotle does not present the acquisition of virtue as satisfaction. There is of course a desire for the happiness brought by the virtuous life, which he calls '*eudaimonia*', meaning flourishing or happiness. But *eudaimonia* reflects the particular (partial) conditions of human nature, particularly the capacity to exercise practical reason. It is not achieved by escaping or transcending the human condition. Satisfaction comes by exercising practical reason excellently. It is exercised within its limits, not by achieving limitlessness. Moreover, the acquisition of virtue in concrete reality will always be different in each case. What is excellent will differ according to different contexts, with different sets of responsibilities. Virtue is the mean between opposing tendencies and that biting-point is always relative to specific circumstances, not attained by leaving one's circumstances behind. Seeking to transcend limitations and glimpse some broader totality thus runs counter to lasting and enduring happiness, for Aristotle.

By making satisfaction itself literally the 'be all and end all', it is not enough to satiate desire relatively like Aristotle. It is not enough to strike a mean as best you can under the given circumstances. You must aim for the Absolute, for total satisfaction. Otherwise it is just like eating well at dinner and pretending your stomach won't be rumbling for breakfast in the morning. Herein lies the point of connection between political and spiritual Boomerism. Each are acts of rebellion, of dishonour. The first rebels against a society that is so tiresomely imperfect. Rather than take the rough with the smooth and achieve what attainable improvements one can, it desires a world in which everything is unendingly perfect. The second rebels against the fact our desires are never enduringly satisfied, so it desires a world without desire and pretends this is detachment from desire itself. Human nature is always limited and lacking. To pretend otherwise is a dishonour to our humanity.

The pipeline from longing for a political to a spiritual satiation of desire finds its fullest exemplification in Richard Wagner, specifically *The Valkyrie* of *The Ring Cycle*. Wagner saw this cycle as a *Gesamtkunstwerken* or 'total work of art'. It could take the place once held, in times allegedly less sophisticated than his own, by the Christian liturgy. It would be an aesthetic work that somehow contains and drives the impulses behind all the limited and fragmentary others, from whence the very springs of life flow forth from the unseen world, configuring and directing society towards that which is holy.

It is well documented that Wagner became disillusioned with his revolutionary past while working on *The Valkyrie*. At the same time, he became fascinated by the idea of detachment from the world. He also discovered the philosophy of Arthur Schopenhauer. For Schopenhauer 'total reality' is a vast unseen reality which we experience only a tiny part of, through sense experience. Yet music provides a voice for the vast unseen which we would not otherwise know. Wagner's diaries state, 'those seeking in philosophy their justification for political and social agitation' will find in Schopenhauer 'no sustenance whatsover'. Rather, he says Schopenhauer calls for 'the absolute renunciation' of worldly, political desire. As put by Brian Magee, the effect on Wagner was such that '[t]he revolutionary on fire with a mission to save the world had become a rejector of the world'.[4] In terms of the effect on *The Valkyrie*, Magee states, this forsaking of the world enabled the expression of a 'disconcerting emotional nakedness', in which 'forbidden emotions are given open voice, so that what reaches us in the audience is something that has never before found expression in art'.[5] By forsaking his concern for improving conditions in the partial world of everyday experience, Wagner seemed to have unleashed the something from the great totality, 'an inexhaustible seam of feeling buried so deep and under such pressure, as to be dangerous to get near'.[6]

In Wagner's composition of *Tristan and Isolde*, his giving voice to the great totality reaches its climax. For Schopenhauer, music was not the only way human beings might glimpse the great unseen world. The other is sex. In a loving sexual relationship, 'the barriers and limitations of selfhood are transcended, the individual loses his sense of self and experiences oneness with the other person in the sexual act'.[7] A sense of total surrender is something C. S. Lewis connected with erotic love, bringing a preoccupation with the beloved 'in her totality'. This has of course been traditionally expressed by requiring a 'total commitment' on the part of the lover.[8] Such totality has a metaphysical and cosmic framework for Schopenhauer. He understood the unseen force of all reality to be a blind 'will to live', 'the dumb urge to existence'.[9] Sex is doubly important for Schopenhauer because it is bound up with the will to live through procreation. He writes, 'the most intimate knowledge of that inner essence of the world ... the will to live, is to be found' in the 'ecstasy' of 'the act of copulation'.[10] *Tristan and Isolde* is entirely focused on a moment of orgasmic release with the final chord, the point of satisfaction, resolving all the meandering discords of the preceding hours-long work. At the opera's close, the 'inner essence of the world' is disclosed, as with Capra's vision by the ocean.

Considering total satisfaction to be something humanly graspable connects to some of the worst elements of contemporary Western cultures. It helps explain why pornography sinks ever lower in an accelerated descent of ever more extreme acts, because people are trying to find the point of total satisfaction. This is why increasingly bizarre and complex forms of penetration and reception abound, involving ever more chillingly perverse scenarios. When satisfaction is premised on taking hold of the totality of something, the overarching tendency is towards objectification. An object can be totally known, it can be entirely dominated, abused, broken down and discarded at will. Even what is taken to be 'true love' today is still often objectification. It is just changed to treating others as if they were precious objects. That is, taking care not to cause any damage, psychological or physical. A person is objectified when they become a tool for the satisfaction of the other person's desire. Then they are not being treated as a person, as an end in themselves, but as a means for the satisfaction of desire.

Traditionally, personhood is often centred in the bearing of free will. Against the tide of objectification, free will is held up as a sea-wall to hold back the incoming oceanic tsunami of unrestrained desire. Then sexual ethics focus on consent. Ethical and legal debates ensue about whether to consider the dishonest ways men gain consent as forms of sexual violence. Consent alone threatens not to protect against objectification. 'He got me to say yes but I didn't know what I was saying yes to', means 'even my free will became a tool, an object, something to be manipulated for the satisfaction of his desire'.

To consider culture pornified is not about quibbling over gyrating women in G-strings on Breakfast TV. It points to scorched cultural retinas, affecting the way people view the world and live their lives. There is a difference of degree, not of kind, between what the dominant culture considers to be healthy or unhealthy satisfaction. This is the spectrum of degree between a worthless and a precious object. This even applies to the most sinister elements of a pornified culture.

Between child and adult there is the greatest disparity of power, which, if abused, leads to the most wretched, perverse and destructive domination of another person. The child's vulnerability is total. There is no worse dishonour to human nature than to objectify a child for the gratification of desire.

The satirical magazine *Private Eye* used to point out the hypocrisy of media outlets celebrating paparazzi shots of teenage celebrities on one page, with a furious report about a paedophilic crime on another. The tabloids were happy to celebrate the objectification of youthful girls, while simultaneously describing those who commit the most wretched acts as 'monsters'. The word monsters means that those criminals are of a different kind of being to normal people. But what if those people commit deeds which are an intensification of more normalized behaviours, albeit in an appallingly perverse form? The same truth could apply even to the broader culture. Perhaps this is why, if the allegations against Michael Jackson are true, he could be an immensely popular figure and villainous monster at the same time, as was Jimmy Savile. Celebrity itself is a form of objectification. Celebrities desire to be objectified by the masses. They are those for whom honouring people as persons has lost all significance. A celebrity culture is an orgy of shadow chasing, where people yearn for others to desire a mere shadow or visage of their person.

The world of fantastical shadows promises to be a perpetual Neverland of unending possibility. Everyone yearns for a greatness they feel destined to achieve in a world where reality is there for your satisfaction. We'll all land on the world-changing business idea or wake up one day as a global celebrity. Wishes becoming the real inadvertently feed into social phenomena like the fantastical bargaining of OCD or the unreality of body dysmorphia. Certain techniques for dealing with these things threaten to make them worse, like looking at one's reflection and affirming, 'you're amazing'. The fairytale hero looks into his magic mirror to make things real.

Honouring reality as something more than a vehicle for the satisfaction of desire is closely linked to maturation, specifically the teenage years. Now mass adolescentization is obvious to the point of platitude. It is well articulated by Mark Greif, who stated in *Against*

Everything that youth has now 'become permanent'. He cites MTV as the most 'aggressive promoter of one version of youth as a wholesale replacement of adult life'. It is no coincidence that Greif also describes the effects of intoxication well, saying drink and drugs cause a person to enter 'a realm of free experience' and so 'point to a world a lot looser and more liberal than this one'. He is also right to link what he calls the 'lure of a permanent childhood' as 'a vain pursuit of absolute freedom', with a sinister, sexual infatuation with youthfulness. The word 'play' is today itself now sexualized, as with the 'play party', or when preceded by the prefix fore-. But what about the after? The one asking this seems morbid and glum for those trying to live forever on the shadowy promise of a never-arriving total *petit mort*. Wishes and reality synchronize in the viewing of pornography, when images of real (for the most part) people are invited to inhabit the internal space of imagined fantasy. Surrounded by shadows, the perpetual teenager plays with himself.

When Greif tries to articulate ways of healing infantilized adults and sexualized children, however, he claims the 'de-emphasis of sex and the denigration of youth will have to start with an act of wilful revaluation'. We'll have to choose to reprogram ourselves, he says, to prefer 'the values of adulthood: intellect over enthusiasm, autonomy over adventure, elegance over vitality, sophistication over innocence'. This is someone who believes limits can be transcended by yet another act of choice, a concerted desire to make the unending Mardi Gras more humane and palatable. Then people might distinguish between some grotesque acts as liberating, while holding that others are strictly off-limits. 'Love is the law', they'll say, but this is still what Aleister Crowley called 'love under will', safeguarded by consent or, rather, 'wilful revaluation'.

Our contemporary *Boomerdämmerung* is like an unending production of *Tristan and Isolde*, caught up in that fixated state of suspense endlessly chasing its climax. Contemporary life can feel like a grim *Gesamtkunstwerken*, transfixed by the promise of disembarking on a resolutory chord bringing eternal rest. We find ourselves like the escapees who jumped from the Mutiny of the *Bounty* and gave way to the urge to slake their thirst by drinking from the ocean. The salt water diet makes them ever more thirsty, until they are driven mad by their thirst and it steadily destroys them. The preoccupation with the oceanic expanse is not the solution to desiring, it is the exact opposite. The desire for the totality is the unslakeable thirst, which, the more it is cultivated, will intensify itself to the point of madness. Much of *Tristan* is set in Cornwall, the Atlantic Ocean is ever roaring in the background, the great Oneness behind and before all things, ever on the horizon, ready to engulf us into the great totality.

In 1999 there was a solar eclipse, which could be viewed in its entirety, its totality, from this same region of England, Cornwall. Viewing the 'total eclipse' of the sun by the lunar orb is a dramatic cosmic spectacle and a great number of people planned the trip to the West Country to glimpse the totality. Cornwall itself has plentiful esoteric associations. There are ancient standing stones, circles and wells. There are links with the legends of Atlantis, a submerged city miles out to the west of Britain now lost below the ocean. There is also the Arthurian tradition, of Merlin and Morgan Le Fey, Lancelot and Guinevere, as well as Tristan and Isolde. Against this esoteric background, all manner of cranks claimed there was great significance in Cornwall being the site from whence the sun would be seen engulfed by the moon. The sun often represents rationality, order and light in the ancient myths. The moon, by contrast, represents the dark and disordered 'will to live' of biological nature, the 'dumb urges' that Merlin or Morgan could magically manipulate in the caves below Tintagel, as the sound of the ocean roared through cavernous darkness.

With the so-called Millennium Bug dominating the news, there was an apocalyptic tenor around how the eclipse was approached in popular culture. August is known as the 'silly season' for the UK press, when there is little to report during the Parliamentary Recess, so the tabloids run desperate stories to ensure copy, stories which would never normally make it to print. This meant there was a raft of silly stories in the press in the run up to the eclipse. Some journalists reported that Cornwall did not have the infrastructure for the massive invasion, that the taps would run dry and there could be fatal crushes as people rushed back up the country lanes to civilization, desperate for water. Another claimed that the sheer weight of so many visitors to the county would cause a tectonic collapse, that Cornwall had so many abandoned tin-mines under the earth that the sheer weight of thousands upon thousands of people would cause the land to fall in. It would be another Atlantis, when the ocean was no longer held back by the rocky cliffs that had tumbled to the ground. Visitors could find themselves trapped and drowning in Merlin's caves at the precise moment the sky was engulfed in darkness.

Some more alternative commentators said this was a planetary alignment which would usher in the Age of Aquarius, others that this was the first showings of an Aeon of Shiva. Some said the old order, represented by the sun, would finally be crushed by the great lunar forces of disorder. Some saw this as a moment whereby sexual desire could be liberated, just as the Boomers had claimed with 'free love' in the 1960s. Eclipse enthusiasts are called 'shadow chasers' and committed shadow chasers were travelling from all over the world to behold the totality. They were joined by more opportunist shadow chasers, all the cranks and esotericists, hippies and new-agers.

The wealthier cranks competed for deluxe beachside villas. These had inflated rental prices premised on their unbeatable cliff-top vantage points to see the eclipse. There the enlightened ones could perform yogic or tantric rituals, contorting themselves into the opti-mum position for the inflow of cosmic force at the point the totality was revealed. Their baggy silken trousers would faintly quiver with the gentle Atlantic breeze blowing over their bodies as they were carried off into the oceanic ether by cosmic ecstasy. The less wealthy cranks were happy to camp out on the cliffsides and the moors, with only campfires and booze for comfort.

Sure enough, nothing much happened. If there were any archetypes on display that August morning, it was of an archetypal anti-climax. The climax was never reached, because it was a grey, overcast day. The totality could not be seen. Nothing in the sky could be seen, except unremarkable, murky cloud covering everything. The nadir of the anti-climax came when it gradually threatened to rain, turned cold, and then some light drizzle blew in with the chill from the coastline. The hugely disproportionate hype was engulfed, not by the oceanic tide of cosmic ecstasy, but by the boring old English summer rain. The roar of unrestrained Atlantean desire was beaten off with the gentle pitter-patter of the drizzle landing on people's umbrellas and cagoules. Mysterious Cornwall seemed like any other county in less mystical parts of the country. The same roadsigns, the same garages, the same wet concrete smell on the roads. Clustered about were huddles of people who did not quite look like mystical initiates of the unseen world. They just looked like middle-class thrill seekers in waterproof clothes and silly cardboard glasses meant to provide protective sheaths for those UV rays that never came, remaining flaccid among the clouds.

But when these people returned home, many of them were surprised at what they heard. Those who were not shadow-chasing reported strange moments of profundity on the morning of the eclipse. The rest of England had been granted a glorious summer's day, beautiful blue sky without so much as a wisp of cloud. Those who stayed at home glanced upon the partial alignment, took themselves out to the garden or a local park and sat for a few moments feeling the warmth of the sun ever so slightly wane on their skin as the moon covered a segment of the sun. It was a peculiar experience, they said, in which they found themselves taking a few moments of recollection and pondering the mysteries of human existence, of our tiny place in the cosmos. When the black arc of the moon slipped away again, the sun seemed to beat all the more invigoratingly, warming their souls. Then they returned to work, to their chores, or to attending to their children, with a slight sense of adjustment in the atmosphere. They felt something guiding them, something blessing them in their daily deeds.

The great totality is not ours for the having. Honouring this fact frees us to cherish those things apportioned to us; not neglect, escape or otherwise dishonour them. Honouring the fact that reality cannot be ordered around satisfying one's own desire frees you to honour other people, precisely as persons. That is, persons irreducibly different to you, bearers of freedom just like you. Persons who cannot be engulfed into some One, because they too are ends in themselves. 'Love, honour and obey' was once included in the marriage rite, but is now shortened often to 'love and honour'. 'Obey' is seen as too toxic today, too open to abuse, and something to which people cannot relate. But the three elements here are sequential. Love is tempered by honour, whereby the other person is never someone you can possess in his or her totality. The 'totalizing' tendencies of love are restrained by honouring the other person as an end in his or herself. 'To obey' can be seen as flowing from this, for in it is a negating of the will in concrete situations, of any attempt to make the other person fit into your own schemes, the satisfaction of your own self-centred desire. You honour that which is irreducibly different from yourself. Honouring makes love holy, in the sense of holiness as being 'set apart'. The other person is 'set apart' from a world with yourself at its centre: two becoming one in flesh, each having sacrificed their self-centredness to join with the other.

This oneness is a partial and relative oneness, not subsumption into the One. Honouring the One in relation to romantic desire takes shape, not by rudely trying to transport yourself to heaven with quivering ecstasy, but by honouring the one person you are committed to in the *monos* of monogamy. Because the totality of the person should only be honoured, never grasped for one's own ends, it requires a sacrificial commitment that is not provisional – not conditioned by your ever-changing desires or wants – but permanent, indissoluble.

Moreover, all of this was once a mere foreshadowing and preparation for a further negation of self-centredness in rearing a family. Conception is now commonly orchestrated and arranged in way that most aligns with people's desires, to happen at the optimum occasion relative to individuals' career ambitions. But if people must insist on getting mystical about sex, surely it isn't that 'the ecstasy of copulation' gives voice to the inner-workings of reality, but that the miracle of another human life might be entrusted to you, to be honoured and to honour you in return. But, as Joseph Sobran states, children are often assumed to be 'uninvited guests' in today's approach to sex.[11] Traditionally, a couple who would not welcome the conception of life, at least in principle, were seen as unable to welcome each other into their hearts. Here there is a honourable difference of degree. Honouring another person with indissoluble commitment is a precondition for family life because it de-centres oneself. In this decentring is a great loss of control. Accepting the other person, come what may. This loss of control brings freedom, perhaps. A freedom to join with that person, unshackled from the desire for them to fit into your schemes. A freedom to be yourself without being conscripted into theirs. This is the freedom by which love warms your soul as you go about your daily deeds.

5

Obligation

In 1979, Chicago's 97.9 WLUP radio station decided to switch from playing rock to playing disco. Their breakfast DJ, Steve Dahl, was told to start playing disco music or get fired. Dahl responded by leading a 'Disco Sucks' campaign against this new genre of music. The Chicago White Sox were scheduled to play a two-game match against the Detroit Tigers at Comiskey Park stadium on 12 July. The White Sox owner was trying to boost lacklustre numbers at the stadium by arranging increasingly outlandish entertainment. He booked Dahl to lead what was billed as a Disco Demolition Derby in the interval between the two games. Fans were invited to bring disco records to the game, have them dumped in a crate on the pitch and then watch Dahl himself blow the crate up with dynamite.

An attendee bringing a disco record to the game could gain entrance for 98 cents. The enticement worked. Average attendances at Comiskey Park usually ran to about 5,000, but that night over 50,000 showed up. Things soon got out of hand. After Dahl detonated the explosives, excitement boiled over and thousands stormed the pitch. Anarchic scenes ensued, with people stamping on the molten debris of the vinyls, lighting fires, digging up the pitch, destroying the batting cage and climbing up the foul poles. The commentator Harry Caray took to the loudspeaker to urge people to return to their seats, but was ignored. The police eventually turned up in full riot gear and cleared the pitch. By then the damage was so bad the game was forfeited by the White Sox and the Tigers went home victorious.

The Disco Demolition Derby riot was revisited by various commentators on its fortieth anniversary. Discussions of it were caught between two different interpretations. Or rather, discussions of it should have been caught between two different interpretations, but it wasn't that simple. On the one hand, the Derby is interpreted as the

result of unfortunate circumstances. It is seen as significant only insofar as baseball games are rarely forfeited by public disorder. An ESPN
mini-documentary of the evening takes this approach, as indeed does
Steve Dahl himself. This interpretation maintains that Midwesterners
were just weary of disco's overexposure, that the security at Comiskey
Park was insufficient for a crowd of that size, the alcohol was too
cheap, stadium staff were unprepared and the police arrived too late.

On the other hand, the Disco Demolition Derby has been interpreted along identitarian lines. This approach sees it as an explosion
of racism and homophobia. Disco originated in black and Latino
cultures and was the music of choice of New York gay clubs. This
interpretation maintains that white Midwesterners were fearful of
an insurgent black subculture and the increasing visibility of gay
people in the years following the Stonewall riots. This line of thinking
is usually connected with disco's importance for the development
of Chicago's house music scene in the mid 1980s. The Comiskey
Park riot is presented as a moment when disco was forced back
underground, before re-emerging in a different form, fuelled by newly
affordable drum machines and synthesizers. Disco's demise around
the turn of the decade had led some big-name DJs from the New York
meccas like Studio 54 to move to residencies in Chicago clubs, which
then became melting pots for the morphing of the new sound.

The documentary film *Disco Inferno* has a Historian of Sexuality
saying that white, straight America was struggling with the fact that
the 'culture they feel identified with' was 'being marginalized and limited'. Whether or not this is correct – whether Dahl was spearheading
a wave of prejudice – is not the primary issue here. What is of interest
is that no proponent of the identitarian interpretation seems even to
have asked this question. It has become the received account of what
happened and is repeated uncritically ad infinitum. But there are
questions worth asking. How was media negativity towards disco significantly different to punk, heavy metal or even rock 'n' roll? Hip-hop
was shortly afterwards to become one of the most successful music
genres in history and didn't cause any rioting at baseball games. If
Steve Dahl was racially motivated, why did he mock the Bee Gees and
John Travolta? His own mock-disco novelty record 'D'ya Think I'm

Disco?' is a pastiche of Rod Stewart. He was a shock-jock, celebrating the scruffy and raucous culture of late 1970s rock. So he poured scorn on *Saturday Night Fever*'s three-piece white suits, the pina coladas, the stylized and rehearsed dance moves. Dahl's target might just have been a commercial caricature of authentic disco, the pop tunes he would be forced to play, not the 12"s of Brooklyn loft parties or the Paradise Garage.

The identitarian interpretation does not even countenance the possibility of an alternative view. It is a perpetuated monologue echoed by many voices in succession, not a dialogue or conversation between voices taking different positions. But those who take the first interpretation – who see it as a mere combination of unfortunate circumstances – do enter into dialogue with the identitarians. In the ESPN report, for example, the White Sox press office commented in a way that, presumably, those involved in the disco sucks campaign didn't need to in the late 1970s. They said, 'We remain proud of our franchise's long-standing record on advocating for inclusion and diversity.' Steve Dahl himself also acknowledges the other interpretation. He completely dismisses any allegations of racism or homophobia and states: 'Perception is not always reality. Especially when that perception uses the prism of today to look at events forty years ago.' One side acknowledges the existence of the other and situates itself in relation to it. But the other side seems unaware that another perspective exists and just continues the same old line.

Documentaries about the genesis of house and techno music, like *Pump Up the Volume* and *I Was There When House Took Over the World*, are typical examples of the second interpretation. Both show the early house music producer Vince Lawrence talking about his experiences as a steward at Comiskey Park that night. He says the records being thrown onto the crate were not just disco, but all sorts of black music by artists like Marvin Gaye. Vince Lawrence's account seems unrefutable. He was actually there on the stands, while none of the commentators on either side seems to have taken the trouble to find any of the original attendees. His account is authoritative because, unlike the Historian of Sexuality or most of the marketing team in the White Sox press office, when an African American says it felt racially targeted seeing Marvin Gaye records getting blown up, we are obliged to take heed. It is his lived experience. It has an irrefutability that no protestations by Dahl or the White Sox can undo.

Events happen. Representations of those events proliferate through different media. The differing representations are apprehended by people occupying varied perspectives. Those occupants then draw diverse conclusions about what originally happened. We can only see the objective past through the perspective of our subjective present. The clear light of truth strikes the present moment like a ray of light striking a prism. It refracts into a multi-coloured spectrum. To occupy only one place on that spectrum is to be bathed in one particular colour and then everything in sight is coloured the same way. A monotone orientation gives rise to monologue discourse.

By acknowledging that everything in your own perspective is coloured by that perspective, it becomes possible to accept that there are other perspectives at the horizons of one's own. As has happened with Greenham Common, gazing at history lazily leads people never to see a horizon beyond their own. Then history affirms the status quo, whereas acknowledging other perspectives is the first step towards glimpsing the clear light of objective truth, which, strictly speaking, does not belong exclusively to any one perspective. This glimpsing is interpretation. To interpret is to be between different accounts of a thing, situated from subjectivity in relation to objectivity and surmising how best to aim at the latter. Monologue discourse precludes genuine interpretation, in that the objective is replaced by the authority of one account, of one perspective.

Although we can only see the past through the prism of the present, the Western mind has long since delineated ways by which an interpretive balancing of the facts renders some accounts of things better than others. Interpretation first began to be codified as a 'science' during the Enlightenment. It being a science, meant there were systematic, ordered and transparent means of inquiry by which people could be trained to interpret things more accurately than they would otherwise. Then it was a *sine qua non* that the interpreter put to one side his or her own personal investment in the subject matter, the impressions of his or her own lived experience. If it happened that someone was personally affected by the matters under discussion, that someone would have to adopt a neutral, dispassionate stance to encounter the truth; like a geologist studying rock formations or a biologist with the structure of cells.

This scientific approach to interpretation was named hermeneutics. In some ways, this discipline consciously inverted the presuppositions of the past. The most authoritative texts in premodern Europe were the sacred scriptures. It was once presumed necessary for anyone daring to interpret these texts to live an exemplary life of faith, in Holy Orders. That is, to believe with all their heart and mind, to experience the texts in their lives. Their lives had to be based on those texts if they were to interpret them for others. The Enlightenment paradigm challenged this in the name of objectivity. If you ask a priest or a monk what the Bible means, he could not possibly look at the facts of the case dispassionately, because his whole life depends on a particular way of interpreting it.

With the advent of postmodernity, hermeneutics revised and renovated the importance of personal standpoints for understanding what things mean. The perspectival interpretation was valued again. The philosopher Georg Gadamer had already pointed out that those methods of interpretation deemed 'scientific' – systematic, ordered, transparent approaches – restrain and inhibit a genuinely transformative encounter with a text, prohibiting *tout court* the ways texts lay claim on someone in their concrete situation, changing their views on things, modifying behaviours. For Gadamer, interpretation necessitates some personal investment in the meaning of the text, meaning itself is always meaning for a particular person or community. Some methodologically 'true' meaning of a text in which the interpreter has tried to disappear is not genuine meaning, just a competing hypothesis. In Gadamerian language, purportedly scientific methods define the 'horizon' of knowing at the outset, silencing and shackling 'the horizon of the text', and then parameters for interpretation are set in stone before a book is even opened.

Hermeneutic theorists had noticed how even the most purposefully scientific or 'objective' interpretations still mirror the presuppositions of their interpreters. Attempts to arrive at the objective truth of the historical Jesus in nineteenth-century England, for example, presented Jesus as a civilized gentleman. Attempts from Germany after the First World War, by contrast, presented Jesus as an apocalyptic prophet predicting imminent doom and civilizational collapse. The possibility of achieving any objective interpretation at all was eventually placed in doubt. Our contemporary situation has long since passed the point where a neutral standpoint is deemed unproblematic, any 'view from nowhere'. But a 'view from somewhere' can only be classed as such if there are means to evaluate other views from different somewheres. Otherwise someone's 'view from somewhere' will be presented as authoritative, as something people are obliged to accept as the 'view for anywhere'. Then a particular 'view from somewhere' seizes the authority once held by an unproblematic 'view from nowhere'. Modernity and postmodernity, if pushed to extremes, each break a binary. This binary has two sides, which are both necessary for genuine interpretation. The modern seeks to shut down the side of subjectivity. The postmodern seeks to shut down the side of objectivity. Each obliges interpreters to adhere to their side exclusively, whereas genuine interpretation obliges us to take heed of both sides.

Genuine interpretation is a relation of mutual obligation. The interpreter is obliged to approximate as best as possible to an objective interpretation of events, while simultaneously being obliged to be as attentive as possible to subjective perspectives. Blindness to either one or the other makes one side morph into a pseudo-version of the other. Someone's 'lived experience' is taken as objective truth, or a purportedly objective truth drowns out the reality of human experience. Monotonality has then been mistaken as the clear ray of truth itself.

The agility and elasticity of human interpretive skill then decelerates. The 'being between alternatives', which is required for interpretation, recedes, replaced by 'being the only viable side'. Individual perspectives no longer perceive themselves as such. They then become borderless spaces, inhabited by citizens of anywhere feeling obliged to follow the exclusive law of someone's lived experience. Cries for a world without walls grow ever more fervent. Monologue discourse demands freedom from the noise of neighbouring perspectives, but habitations without walls stretch out in all directions and reverberate back into themselves, hemming people in like black holes in empty space. Black holes suck all the elements within range into the vacuum. A shape without sides is no longer a shape. The meaningless masquerades as the meaningful. The inconsequential becomes the incontestable. Futile projections are mistaken for fecund profundities.

Black holes appear when stars reach the end of their life-cycle. Entropy reaches the nadir of deceleration and the star folds in on itself and burrows a hole into which space and time accelerate. As with stars, so with civilizations. The deceleration of the West folds in on itself, sucks everything in and destroys itself. The woeful state of the identitarian humanities is widely acknowledged. For philosophers like Gadamer, hermeneutics was a shared, foundational commitment of these disciplines, functioning like logic or mathematics do in natural sciences like physics or chemistry. These 'human sciences' are those which seek to articulate human life in its fullness. That is, human life as it is lived, caught between the demands of human perspectives and the demand of objectivity, an objectivity which guarantees their scientific pedigree. The humanities explore and perpetuate the socio-cultural patrimony of their contexts, their perspectives, and find the objectivity therein. Of course, it would be precisely here that Western deceleration would implode into its opposite, the furious nexus of identitarian irreverence. Because here subjectivity seeks after objectivity, it honours both obligations. The most far-reaching recognitions of the perspectival in postmodern philosophy flip back onto themselves, against objectivity. They manifest new monotone mythologies of *Menschlichkeit*.

Once a wormhole opens up, everything within range is sucked in. Identity politics becomes the *raison d'être* of academia itself. No longer concerned with universal knowledge, the formation of character or even striving for the common good, universities claim to exist for the purpose of levelling inequalities of outcome between groups with minority characteristics. The edge of the forcefield around a black hole is the event horizon. Once passed, consumption by the hole is inevitable. Approaching the event horizon everything decelerates, before suddenly inverting and accelerating into its opposite. The event horizon for academia came with the unavoidable pervasiveness of the market, combined with the complex coordinates of technocratic learning. University professionals were being dragged along by the hollow-eyed apparatus which was grinding them down and grinding to a halt, but then it passed the horizon whereby everything careered off into the new promise of meaning: woke activism. The *Boomerdämmerung* is the death of the Western star. Its morbid luminescence radiates the twilight of these times. Strange figures have predicted its appearance for millennia and they trek along the old Silk Road to come and feast on its incandescent bounty.

An event horizon in cosmology has an analogy in the science of interpetation: conversion. This is not merely adjusting and incorporating another's insights into your own worldview. It means a radical change after someone's perspective has been radically altered by a glimpse of something conceived as objective. This is a seeing-of-all-things-differently, from whence there is no return. In postmodernity, the convert is a troublesome, unwelcome figure. The convert says boldly that his or her subjective lived experience was wrong. In practical terms, today's cautious reserve towards conversion has meant people of different religious faiths can explore constructive co-existence in ways once impossible. At the same time, however, expecting believers in a religion like Christianity or Islam to leave their fervour at the door and promise not to try to seek converts, mirrors the totalitarianism of the old Enlightenment science. There is a new authoritative stance, that believers at least act as if their respective views were equally valid, equally binding. An exclusive obligation to lived experience perpetuates what postmoderns would see as the worst sins of the past, just with different blasphemy laws. The forbidden sentiment is the claim to an objectivity binding on a subjective perspective: the claim, 'this is binding upon you'.

Few converts are treated as roughly as those who convert from Judaism to Christianity. In thirteenth-century England, Jewish converts to Christianity were required to submit all their estate to the crown.

Henry III established a house where such converts could then reside, the *Domus Conversorum*, whose warden had the job of archiving and protecting the records of the Court of Chancery. This court was a strange court of appeal, for complex cases which the common law was unable to settle. It thus became known as a court of 'reason', of a sphere of objectivity that somehow transcended common practice, defining exceptions rather than precedents. It is associated with 'conscientious law', calling to mind the medieval teaching on conscience as a sphere of moral objectivity preserved intact after the fall from grace. It is therefore interesting that the keeper of the records of this court doubled as warden for those who had made the unthinkable leap of conscience by becoming converts. This place was the meeting point of two sides to obligation. Controversies from different particular perspectives unresolved by the common law were here met with the binding objectivity of a final settlement. With converts, those whose religious and cultural perspective was found untenable resided in the bosom of that which rescinded it, in a Christian community with its own chapel.

Over the centuries the use of the *Domus Conversorum* to keep the records of the Court of Chancery took precedence over the housing of converts, until it became just a place where court records were kept. The Warden was also called 'Master of the Rolls', for he kept the administrative record of the Chancery Court on rolls of parchment. This role developed until many centuries later, in the mid nineteenth century, it had responsibility for the Public Records Office. On a site adjacent to the chapel of the *Domus Conversorum* a municipal building was constructed to house the Records, which opened in 1858. In the last years of the nineteenth century the remains of the chapel were enclosed within the Public Records Office. The Public Records Office was transformed into an academic library and reopened in 2001, housing the humanities and law collections for King's College London.

Archiving as a concept contains within it a commitment to the mutually conditioning obligations of objectivity and subjectivity. Archives are kept for posterity, so people might know how things came to be the way they are. But that knowledge is always knowledge for a particular situation, a particular set of questions or controversies, and thus related to subjectivity. Having archives available, moreover, is a commitment to further questions in developing situations, to ongoing discovery from different interpretations arising in different times and places. The existence of archives is therefore prefaced on the mutual obligation to subjectivity and objectivity. In the meeting of these authoritative interpretation is to be found. Heeding obligation thus gives rise to authority, not the other way round.

Yet authority is today deemed inherently problematic. So it comes as no surprise that archiving itself is problematized in postmodern philosophy. Jacques Derrida's *Archive Fever* draws our attention to the etymological route of the term 'archive'. The Greek *arkhé* means both 'origin' or 'beginning' and 'power'. In the first usage, this is the word used for the 'beginning' of 'In the beginning was the Word' of John's Gospel. In the second, it comes down to us in words such as hier-archy. For Derrida, an archive is related to 'origin' insofar as it contains the records of a thing deemed original and closest to the original occurrence. But archives are inseparably related to power insofar as what is deemed 'original', what is made available and to whom it is made available are defined by who is in power. To construct, preserve and guard the archives, he says, is to 'have the power to interpret the archives'.[1] The kernel of truth here is that power dynamics do affect the way people know things and, of course, anyone who has lived in a totalitarian regime can verify that the dispensation of, and access to, past histories is tightly controlled. Derrida connects the 'origin' aspect of the word 'archive' to the word 'commencement' and the 'power' side to the word 'commandment'.

Derrida claims that archiving controls commencement by means of commandment. Access to the records deemed closest to the original occurrence reflects the whims of whoever is in power. He calls the commandment or power side to this the 'nomological', from *nomos* meaning 'law'. Those with legal authority command full obligation, therefore, over truth itself. The link between subjectivity and objectivity is broken. That deemed objective or 'original' is controlled by the subjective present, by 'power'. But before the postmodern era, the concept of 'law' was not tainted by such cynical presuppositions.

The sphere of human law was tethered to a more ultimate law, a law human beings do not invent, but which they discover. This would include natural law and what is sometimes called the moral law. A residual trace of it is found in liberal democracies that make space for a 'conscience vote' in the legislature. This vote cannot be compelled on the basis of party allegiance, for each person is answerable to a higher authority. It can thus be called 'conscientious law', like that exercised through the Courts of Chancery, the records of which were kept in the *Domus Conversorum*.

That human laws were once seen as rooted in a higher law explains to some extent why jurisprudence was originally considered a humanities discipline. As put by the nineteenth-century philosopher Wilhelm Dilthey, law is based on a 'sense of justice' which arises in 'lived experience', from which 'belief in a higher order' derives. Dilthey did not mean the higher order or moral law is not real or not genuinely transcendent, just that it enters consciousness when people feel something to be just or unjust in their lived experience. This experience crystallizes through a widespread human impulse to construct systems of earthly law, to have a just legal framework. But, for Dilthey, this framework can only ever codify specific instances and guidelines for applying the moral law itself, relative to concrete circumstances. Much of the moral law is too profound, or too abstract or too distant in divine origin to be crudely transposed into human law while remaining universal for all contexts. In this classical understanding of law, what is most appropriate for a given situation, the particular, meets the best approximation of what the moral law demands, the universal. Mutual obligation is bound up with traditional jurisprudence.

In Dilthey's time, jurisprudence was an exemplar of a humanities discipline for precisely this reason. A humanities subject, by definition, is one that must not swamp particular subjective perspectives with universally valid or objective laws. But neither can it so emphasize subjectivity that scholars of these disciplines can forsake or forget the demands of objectivity. A natural scientist will here retort that natural science does not simply swamp the particular with the universal. New findings from microscopes and telescopes reveal new particularities from whence modified understandings of laws are attained. But the primary outcome of natural science, at least in Dilthey's day, was simply the laws themselves, the objectivity of which no longer needs to interplay with subjectivity.

Let us take the example of a person reading a book of poems. The natural scientist sees the book as a chemically constructed physical object, the constituents and interrelating of which can be reduced to the elements of the periodic table. This book is apprehended through the senses, the lawful activity of which is defined by human biology. Biology and psychology can offer conclusions onto how the inner impressions caused by the poems rely on human capacities for language comprehension and emotional reflexes to stimuli. This explains the scene of someone reading a book of poems.

Seeking to understand the scene in the manner of Dilthey, however, would seek only to describe the scene as it is undergone. This involves not grounding the scene on what he would call the 'heuristic constructions' of natural science, like the chemical formulae of the components of the paper and ink or inferred properties of humanity such as language comprehension and emotional reflexes. Rather, Dilthey would seek to articulate as accurately as possible the actual experience of the person reading the poems, not explaining why the impressions are given as they are, but articulating their specific character. These impressions will be deeply personal and so Dilthey's method involves understanding human beings in their subjectivity.

Yet Dilthey considers demands of universality and objectivity always to bear on our understanding of things. Someone reading a book of poems can enter in and experience those poems because human subjectivities have the capacity for mutual understanding, for being taken out of their own subjectivity and into the mind of another. The greatest expressions of humanity are those which can carry a multitude of subjectivities with them. The greatest art aims at universality the most successfully. You do not need to be an eighteenth-century Viennese to enjoy Beethoven's symphonies, nor an English Elizabethan to enjoy the plays of Shakespeare. Something objectively good pertains to such art, so it speaks to people from radically different contexts.

The key point for Dilthey is that there is no stable, universally valid, law that defines how and why human expressions in music or drama have this effect. The laws of chemistry or biology cannot do it justice or, to put it better, they cannot capture 'why' certain expressions have this quality and others do not. In his own example, Dilthey says that on hearing the final note of Beethoven's Fifth Symphony, an audience member cannot explain why it had to end with this note; but he or she knows with indubitable certainty that it *should* have ended this way. In fact, it feels that it *had* to; this is an objective truth. This 'should' is universal and objective, yet it makes no sense to remove it from the particular and subjective experience of hearing it. You cannot describe or articulate it without heeding both obligations, there is no abstractly lawful objectivity existing on its own plane. Both sides are required; finding the truth of the matter involves heeding the obligations of each.

Dilthey states that the 'final goal of the human sciences' is 'the understanding of concrete history in its complexity'. One of his key concepts is what he calls 'lived experience', which is life as it is lived in this 'concrete history'. It is complex because, in lived experience, people may never sever the 'bond between the singular and the universal'.[2] The experiencing of human life is always happening through subjectivity, but that subjectivity is always discerning how an experience might apply to other experiences, including the experiences of other people, and ultimately seeking what is objectively true. The capacity for subjectivities to speak across different contexts is seen by Dilthey as a defining feature of humanity, something not granted to other species. The humanities are formalized and specialized disciplines, which grow organically from the reality of lived experience. Dilthey's approach to 'lived experience' is foundational for the human sciences, but put to one side in natural science. He writes, 'History, political events, the sciences of law and of the state, the study of religion, literature, poetry, architecture, music, of philosophical worldviews and systems' are unlike the natural sciences because they 'emerged naturally from the task of life itself'.[3] This task is the meeting of mutual obligation.

* * *

Dilthey's understanding of the humanities arose in response to intellectual currents of his day. There was firstly the growing authority of natural science, which, were it to conquer human science, would in Dilthey's mind woefully 'truncate' our understandings of the fullness of human life.[4] There was also, secondly, a contemporary of Dilthey's, Wilhelm Windelband, who argued that the difference between natural and human sciences was actually the difference between objectivity and subjectivity. He says the natural sciences disclose universal laws and the human sciences disclose only subjective realities. Dilthey argues that Windelband does a grave disservice to human nature, undermining the foundational ability we have to relate to each other through ideas and the arts.

For Dilthey, 'lived experience' is where human beings take the phenomena of life as real and binding and yet implicitly discern the significance of things by configuring them in relation to more general truths and, ultimately, objective truth. The impression one has from a certain person, if not clearly corroborated by others, might lead you to deem it insignificant. If others agree, however, a general impression is the more persuasive. In dramatic circumstances something unquestionable might arise from such an experience, such as a universally applicable distaste towards dishonest behaviour, for example. This dislike of dishonesty can be entirely understood by someone of a completely different cultural, ethnic or socio-economic background.

Dilthey maintains that in lived experience our first impulse is to accept what we see, think and feel, unquestioningly. The ability to discern objective truth arises from the human being's experience of what he terms 'restraint'. He says the human experience of a world of 'resisting pressures' gives rise to knowing that reality is independent of ourselves, that there is an objective world. This happens most perceptibly when our desires are restrained, when we have an intention that is not realized and the resistance we meet is 'acknowledged as a restraint' of that intention.[5] The German for 'restraint' here is *Hemmung*, of the same root as 'hem in' as in 'to border'. He says that from this experience people can discern the border between 'an outside object and my person'.[6] We have seen that when infantile

experiences of restraint were never fully accepted, there are consequences all through life. Unrestrained desire in adults, we have also
seen, gives rise to a makebelieve world. For Dilthey, it is from the
primordial boundary between ourselves and the world that the ability
to discern objectivity comes into our minds at all. Intellectual activity
is rooted precisely here, from this the humanistic disciplines arise as
things binding on others and not a realm of subjective fancy.

Yet the phrase 'lived experience' is most commonly used today in
a way that ignores one side of Dilthey's analysis, the obligation to
seek objectivity. This slippage has occurred because the humanities
have continued to try to shore up their stability against the natural
sciences by questioning the possibility of objectivity itself. Today's
humanities mirror Windelband exactly. Defenders of the humanities
like Dilthey were those who argued passionately that there are human
universalities, that our lived experiences are broadly comparable one
with another. Human beings relate to each other by definition of
being human. The simple truth at stake then has been expressed by
Thomas Chatterton Williams, saying 'a total stranger who checks
none of the identity boxes you do can nonetheless articulate your
most ineffable aspirations and inner states more clearly than even
your closest kin'.[7]

The identitarian humanities are the result of a surrendering to the
particular on the basis of power dynamics. Lived experience is then
only understood by someone experiencing the same dynamics. We see
this at work today when educationalists argue that schoolchildren of a
particular race must primarily learn the history of that race in school,
otherwise they cannot relate to the discipline of history. The same
idea explains why BBC News tends to have a Northern Irish person
reporting on Northern Ireland, or someone who is mobility impaired
reporting on disability issues. Pushed further, this principle explains
why the #MeToo campaign could call for unconditional belief in an
allegation ('it felt like harassment in my lived experience') and why
mental health discourse can now prohibit ever acknowledging that
people might exaggerate or fabricate suicidal feelings. The prevalence of the term 'gaslighting' is a case in point. Disagreeing with
someone's interpretation of things, voicing a different perspective,

can now be considered emotional abuse. This is instructive, because emotional abuse causes a person's grip on reality to break down. If this breakdown of reality happens over differences of opinion, people are applying subjective opinions to all of reality.

There are some points of resistance to the relativizing of all things under the rubric of lived experience. Yet some of those defending objectivity would gain much from Dilthey's philosophy. They often exclusively hold to the objectivity of natural science and downplay the particularity of subjective experiences, they replay the broken binary of modernity against that of postmodernity. Helen Pluckrose and James Lindsay argue that we need a 'mass commitment to the universally liberal principles and the rigorous, evidence-based scholarship that define modernity'.[8] A return to the Enlightenment is needed, we read, to recover 'belief in objective knowledge, universal truth, science (or evidence more broadly) as a method for obtaining objective knowledge' (original parentheses).[9] However, the understanding of science or evidence in this argument does not and cannot contain the complexity of the human sciences. What evidence is there to explain why Goethe is more compelling than Hollywood blockbusters viewed by millions more people than those that have read *The Sorrows of Young Werther?*

Pluckrose and Lindsay say the difference between experience and facts is 'not particularly mysterious'. It is just 'the difference between knowing that and knowing how', knowing that something is the case compared to knowing how it is experienced.[10] This gets to the very nub of what Dilthey wants to say. In phenomena of human expression we cannot do one of these without the other. This is why the human sciences are different. When you hear the last note of Beethoven's Fifth, you know that this is how it should have ended, because this is how you and countless others experience it ending. How something appears in experience can define what that something is. The experiential can define the factual in ways which are objective. These ways, like those in natural science, approximate as best as they can to objectivity. But they are different because they require enduring reference back to experience to make any sense. The human sciences mirror lived experience because they contain both obligations.

The question is whether we can re-learn the science and art of interpretation. It is to ask if our obligations can be heeded, if lines can be drawn in the sand once again. The mark of this beast will be demarcation, its line of approach, delineation. Raving-mad revisionism of history needs to be met with a new sober-minded sagacity. From seeing everything bathed in the colour of a monotone hue, eyes will squint at the clear light of truth and many will choose to crawl back into the twilight. Some, however, will become adepts of starlight. The chapel at the heart of the *Domus Conversorum* will be re-consecrated, people will enter and behold the light once again. Just as the light of the stars we see is hundreds of years old, these adepts of this chapel will guard and transmit the forgotten knowledge of the past, a knowledge that is binding upon all, but can never be unbound from the circumstances where it first came forth. This light casts away the darkness of a truth for anywhere, yet enlightens particular somewheres with a light that shines everywhere.

6

Respect

Refracted light span out from the interpretation of the Disco Demolition Derby at Comiskey Park. It passed through Chicago and Detroit and continued to mutate as it shone in different times and places. In London there were multitudinous rays of this light shining in the early 1990s. An intense period of cultural change occurred as the peoples of the city took the cultural impulses and made them their own. New impulses were fused with the old and a different light would in turn also refract to be viewed one-sidedly on the other side of a prism, some years later.

London's reception of the music of Chicago and Detroit led to significant alterations in how it sounded. It got much faster. Production values decreased as youngsters could now sequence music on cheap home computers. Samplers were the dominant instrument. These use sounds from other music, they do not create new sounds with keyboards or drum machines. The new music was made purely by editing pre-existent material. Composition now meant cutting, slicing, fusing, slowing-down or speeding up sounds from records and films. Composers now just played with whatever knobs and dials might force one sound to fit with another. The result was a collage of sheer derivation; a work of art in which every element was derived from sources other than the artist. Yet it would be wrong to judge this music as imitative. It employed diverse elements from elsewhere – beats from hip-hop, elongated basslines from reggae and bleepy techno sounds – yet the end result sounded nothing like any of these genres.

The elements all derived from elsewhere, but the final product was unique to its own time and place. It is no exaggeration to say this music sounded like a demented noise to someone encountering it for the first time back then. It defied categorization entirely. To listen to it, your ears had to forget the derivations, stop trying to make sense of the familiar bits. It was necessary to avoid trying to categorize the different elements at play, but to allow a coherence to emerge from the amalgamation of sounds. There was a distinct coherence, if you could let the alterations and reconfigurations of the original sounds be heard together.

The music was mostly produced in teenagers' bedrooms and then cut onto white-label 12" records for a few hundred pounds at local pressing plants in industrial estates to the north and east of the city centre. The outpourings of sounds of the bedrooms were played 24 hours a day on a range of pirate radio stations with transmitters erected illegally on London's tower blocks. These radios had adverts every hour or two calling listeners to attend club nights or one-off parties in rented warehouses or leisure centres.

Living in an area of London where this subculture had taken hold during this period, the deafening staccato beats and rumbling basslines would be emitted by passing cars every few minutes. Going from one end of the FM dial to the other, there would be numerous junctures where white noise gave way to this music pouring out from the pirate radios. It would be accompanied by the voice of someone shouting along with the music; showing appreciation for a particular tune or passing on messages from one person to another, which had been phoned in from listeners via a pager.

Older kids and adults would attend the nights where the music was played every Friday and Saturday. Younger kids just had the radio, and cassettes borrowed from their peers, which had been copied from older brothers and sisters before being passed around school. Like any subculture, the scene developed its own internal language, coded signifiers showing who was familiar with it and who was not. Listening to a pirate radio on a Friday or Saturday night, the enthusiasm and energy of the music and the voices grew as the clock turned towards midnight, when people would start venturing out. By 6am the music and voices would be more tranquil and would stay as such until mid morning, while the partygoers were coming home to get some sleep. It would then pick up again in the late afternoon.

* * *

Thirty years later, the chroniclers of British popular music write of this scene with great respect. This is particularly true of certain clubs. The music press now features potted histories of what are considered 'legendary' venues, where this new sound was forged, or produce documentaries interviewing the club's founders about its early years. But during their heyday, these clubs got no respect from the respectable quarters of the music press. The scene was intensely popular – the music would be heard not just from passing cars, but from houses with an open window on the first floor, in shops with young staff and, at night, from quaking buildings with masses of partygoers gathered outside on the street. But the scene was deemed to be intensely unfashionable by those who wrote for the music magazines and the supplements of the weekend papers. On the rare occasions when it was mentioned there, it was condemned. The music was written off as poorly produced, naff and crudely formed, as having no real composition or originality. It was dismissed as cheaply made 'recession music'. The phrases and manners of speaking of the voices on the radios were mimicked with phonetic spelling, mocked as yobbish shouting and incomprehensible gibberish. The nights out were belittled for being full of drugged-up kids and violent thugs.

The more mature sounds of the Chicago and Detroit of the 1980s, by contrast, were now ultra-fashionable. This was the music played in the more well-to-do clubs of Soho or Covent Garden, venues with dress codes to keep out the rabble from the ghettos. They used cleverly ironic images for their publicity, to ensure only a suitably knowing crowd would attend. The music of these clubs was billed with qualifiers to differentiate it from the popular variants beloved of the masses: like 'intelligent' house or 'deep' techno. These more select nights and this allegedly more discerning music was written about with great respect by the respectable journalists.

The kids into the harder versions of the music were unaware of all this. They knew only what everyone listened to where they lived, with no care for what people in the nicer parts of town made of it. Young teenagers were happy just to devour the cassette tapes and sounds of the radio. It had plenty of respect in their immediate vicinity, it was fashionable for them. The more concerted enthusiasts among those kids aspired one day to play this music on the radio stations or at the clubs. To do this, plenty of those 12" white labels needed to be acquired. They cost £4 each. They were not sold in high-street music stores, because they had unofficial distribution networks. They had no copyright status, as they lifted sounds and segments from copyrighted music and might attract unwanted attention from the lawyers of the major labels. Those producing the music didn't have the requisite tax status, many of them signed on. So a few hundred quid changing hands here and there between the artist and the buyer all had to be done in cash and kept below the radar.

To say 'distribution network' is misleading. The music was usually distributed by enthusiasts of the music driving around town in a van, having negotiated a cut of the profit with the record's producer, who was himself often skint after getting the thing pressed. A man in a van would turn up at an independent record shop with a box of unmarked 12"s, play one to the owner of the store, who would decide how many to buy for stock, there and then, in cash. Copies had usually been passed to those who played the music at the clubs and on the radio and the more memorable tunes already had an audience ready to buy them before they turned up in the shops. When a tune well-known from the radio was brought into a shop, the staff would buy a good few boxes, confident they could all be sold. There were occasions where the distribution man would put his tune on the record deck to play it to the shop's owner and, within a few seconds, all the punters recognized it and gathered round the counter keenly, wanting to buy it. At the same time as the shopkeeper placed his wad of £20 and £50 notes in the hand of the man supplying the record, he refilled his till with the £5 and £10 notes of the people gathering round the counter to buy it.

These independent shops were a micro-scene in themselves. They were the only place where both the younger and elder aficionados of the scene would be gathered together. Those too young to go to the clubs were alongside those old enough to attend them. While the clubs have entered into the annals of British popular music history, these record shops remain unknown and undocumented. Their particular ray of light has not yet been refracted through the prism of a standpoint situated decades later, today.

There was a specific circuit of such shops which have now all disappeared, as have even the high-street music chains in an age of internet streaming. The shops had an energy and a character all of their own. These were not places where one popped-in to buy a particular record, did a transaction, and then left. Nor were they places to come and browse. The establishments specializing in this genre sold in the back of the shop, in the basement or upstairs on the first floor; anywhere away from the main shopfront. The way these shops functioned required that the music was played, not just bought and sold. The music was meant to be played very loudly. It was played for hours on end at a deafening volume, so the rooms had to be out the way and were often soundproofed. The importance of volume is not about loudness. The key element of the music was the bass frequency and, no matter how loud the volume on a home stereo was turned, it would never capture the body-shaking vibrations in the way a full-sized sound system would. This was the only place where the younger people who did not go to the clubs could hear the music as it was meant to be heard, at a volume impossible to reach in a domestic setting.

To visit one of these shops, it was necessary first to know where the hidden room was. Up a rickety old staircase with a tatty carpet, down some stone steps into a murky basement, or behind a heavy unmarked fire-door out back, from the other side of which cacophonous reverberations broke out whenever someone entered or left. Inside, there would be thick clouds of smoke. There were no shelves with stock, just an empty room with a big high counter running from one side to the other. Behind this counter were cardboard boxes of new records ripped open, sometimes with the name of an artist or a track scrawled on with marker pen. Some records had a stamp on each white label to identify them, made by the artist. All these shops had record decks behind the counter playing the music and massive speakers stacked in piles around the room.

To buy one of the records you had to attract the attention of one of the staff while it was playing and signal to him that you wanted it. This was no easy task. The staff member would often himself be lost in the tune, or busily pulling out the next record from one of the boxes beneath the counter, or in a shouted conversation with a friend on the other side of the counter. But, once the signalling technique had been mastered and a punter knew how to be noticed, that punter would acquire a pile of records while standing at the counter, by gradually collecting those tunes he wanted to buy. The impression on entering was of a group of people just listening to music and socializing. It was more like entering a bar than a shop, as if the ears were taste-buds deciding they wanted a glass of whichever new and exciting brew was being savoured on the tongue, while enjoying the levity it brought them as they imbibed it. There were times when a particular tune was so in demand, the staff behind the counter would just throw a copy on everyone's pile when they arrived, knowing it would be considered worthy of purchase. Or, over time, the staff would know a regular's tastes well enough to put a particular record on his pile when he arrived, knowing he would want to buy it; not needing to wait for his signal.

Late on Friday and Saturday afternoons, many appeared in these shops having just been paid. They came straight from a market stall or building-site down the road or, having just clocked out, from a super-market or warehouse. Their commitment was such that they were happy to part company with their disposable income within minutes of it being laid in their hands, pulling out little brown payday envelopes with fresh notes inside. By contrast, the younger kids in attendance had only pocket money. For them, a visit to one of these shops could go on for hours as they discerned how best they could spend their £10 or £15, on whichever two or three records were deemed most essential. It was rare for anyone to make a quick visit to one of these shops, that was not how they worked. People with cash tended to spend more than they planned. The energy and intensity of the place could lead them to acquire more of this music than they could afford.

These shops were not primarily retail outlets, in the normal sense. They were gathering places, somewhere to go and hang out. Someone without any money could turn up with friends or even alone. After saying 'I'm not buying today', he could still catch up with the regulars and the staff and listen to whatever weird new music had arrived that week. Like the sounds of the pirate radios, these shops grew in intensity at nightfall on the weekends. They rarely opened before noon and they'd be empty till mid afternoon, when punters began to emerge from the night before. By nightfall the room would be full to the rafters, the volume of the music seeming to get louder as the crowd grew in number. On the way back out through the main shopfront, its lights were switched off and the counter closed. Staff would have come out to unlock the front door for people coming and going, like a pub lock-in.

These shops had their own codes of conduct. Those not initiated into how they functioned, even if they could find the room with the counter, would have no idea what to do when they entered it. There were no records to browse, there was no way of getting to the staff and ask them for guidance. Everyone was engrossed in the ritual at the counter. When one of the younger kids arrived for the first time and plucked up the courage to enter after hearing the reverberations inside, he would at first tentatively observe what was going on. He would feign natural and at-ease movements, learning slowly how such a place operated, gradually making his way closer to the counter. Eventually – maybe on the third or fourth visit – he could grab a spot by moving in quickly after someone on the front line nearest to the counter left. Then there was the task of making sure the staff knew he wanted to purchase a particular tune. After many weeks of practice, the same kid would be confident enough to push to the front on entering the shop and confidently mark out his spot. Eventually a staff member might acknowledge his arrival simply by throwing a tune onto his pile without even asking, because he knew it would be to his liking. Well, then he had truly arrived. The record in question would be forever prized among his collection.

These places had their own rituals and practices. It did not matter that this scene was actively disrespected by the respectable. It had generated its own 'habits of respect'.[1] That is, its own internalized practices by which one was treated with due regard, while equally exhibiting due regard for the nature of the place, the manner in which it operated and those who were there. These habits of respect had to be learned. Participation had to be earned. These were not habits artificially imposed by any rulebook or coaching. There was no finishing school to teach someone how to hold themselves, no PowerPoint slides with bullet-point lists of the various dos and don'ts.

These habits of respect were all undocumented and uncodified and they remain so to this day. The habits were gradually engrained on those who participated in them, all of whom had no prior exposure to them, because the concept of the place was novel. Yes, there were elements at play which were derived from other settings. These include the attitude of London's working class towards middle-class manners and etiquette, phrases like 'Excuse me' or 'How can I help you?' There was the traditional Jamaican barber-shop, which was similarly heaving with punters on a Saturday evening, while bass-heavy music shook the room. There was the old wideboy mentality for which wheeling-and-dealing and under-the-counter sales were standard practice. But, while these elements were derived from elsewhere, the end result was not imitative at all. These were places unique to their time and place. They had developed their own habits of respect.

* * *

Now the history of this early 1990s scene is written of fondly by the very music press that disparaged it. These earlier, underground years are presented as the epitome of cool. Yet it is understandable that journalists were initially so critical of this music. It can sound bizarre, at times even ridiculous. Some of those £4 tunes are now regarded as 'seminal classics' and change hands for hundreds of pounds and they still sound as though they've been filtered through a transistor radio, have drum loops out-of-sync with the vocals, or sloppy sound engineering with the levels varying wildly between the different elements at play. To make the vocal samples fit the speed of the music, producers would just crudely speed them up. They could sound like someone playing an old Motown album at 45rpm, the voices like cartoon chipmunks, an ear-piercing, barely recognizable noise. It was as if the sounds had to be coerced, forced into a shape they could not fit, leaving them restrained to the point of mutilation.

At the same time, however, the music can evince real depth. There is an innovative and creative playing with sounds, a genuinely inventive use of syncopation and the running of multiple layers at different speeds. There are haunting and memorable melodies with lush orchestration, the use of technology to provide a soundtrack to the twists and turns of human subjectivity, which traditional instruments music cannot quite capture. Then the mood is not one of restraint, but freedom. The fusing of man and machine seemed to have released something hitherto buried deep within, something that had never had a voice by which to express itself.

These aspects to the music got more prevalent as it developed, as the first generation of producers got more sophisticated and acquired more professional equipment. It could have been this which led the music journalism establishment to change its attitude towards it. By the mid 1990s, those qualifiers once applied only to the original sounds of Chicago and Detroit started to be applied to this younger sibling from London; it could now be 'intelligent' or 'deep'. It was like the first time Wagner's *Tristan and Isolde* was performed. The discords simply couldn't be accommodated by the listeners as they had learned to adjust their ears to a new register. Once they had made this adjustment, new possibilities of musical exploration were suddenly released into the world. Sure enough, the music was eventually re-presented by the press as something worthy of respect after all. The protagonists of its 'intelligent' variants were turned into stars for their magazine covers. It entered the official canon of British popular music.

Perhaps inevitably, the representation and analysis of the scene translated into the mainstream looked somewhat different to the early 1990s heyday. The weekly music papers *NME* and *Melody Maker* and the bumper, glossy monthly magazines like *The Face, Mixmag* and *Select* were all unanimous in what was significant about this new music, as indeed were the entertainment writers at the *Guardian* and *The Independent*. The key characteristic for understanding this thing was the very nexus of what they said gave it meaning and relevance. There was something that meant people should pay great attention to it, they said. This was that it was the first British genre of black music. Before now, the commentators wrote, black music in Britain had been derivative from either the States or the Caribbean, like jazz and hip-hop or reggae and calypso. This music had not only been conceived and gestated in Britain; it was black.

For an afficionado of the earlier scene, it seemed curious that this was the thing reckoned to merit attention, specifically by middle-class, mostly white, journalists. Now they came to mention it, many of the staff and punters in the shops were indeed black. The majority of artists and DJs were too, but nowhere near exclusively so. The clubs could vary quite a lot in whether they pulled a largely black or white crowd. The punters of the music were probably mostly white overall, presumably reflecting the demographics of the time. But it was at first definitely the most popular music of choice for black teenagers, although things had moved on by the time the music press picked up on it. In any case, all the places associated with the scene were to some degree racially mixed.

Musically, there is no doubt the sounds of Chicago and Detroit were altered by the diverse influences of multicultural London. The more polished electronic sounds had been furnished by raw Jamaican elements, particularly. The electronic music developing in Germany or Holland tended to sound mechanized, less soulful, less funky or jazzy. The music had fused with elements of the hip-hop and elec-tro beloved of black teenagers in the 1980s. Notwithstanding this, however, the racial dynamics of this scene did not seem particularly important. It is truer to say that people from outside racialized it, they highlighted the racial dynamics as grounds to leverage respecta-bility. These journalists clearly noticed the numbers of black people at the clubs and found the accents on the radios unfamiliar because they had not heard them before. One could equally have pointed out how influences that could be considered white were prevalent in the music – samples from bands like Kraftwerk, samples of voices with cockney accents, even remastered TV theme tunes like *Emmerdale Farm*.

The question is why it was race, specifically, that gave journalists a rationale for presenting this music scene as worthy of respect after all. To answer this question, some mention should be made of the context in which the music press was writing in the mid 1990s. This was the time of what they liked to call 'Cool Brittania'. To enter into this context, it needs to be understood that the Boomer generation who came of age in the 1960s had not been as influential on British

popular life as their American counterparts. Britain in the 1960s was
not changed to anything like the same degree as the USA. The biggest
changes in Britain happened when a slightly later generation came of
age; a distinctly British variant of the Boomer. This generation has
been described by Ben Sixsmith as those 'born too late for the heydays
of Bob Dylan and Beatlemania but early enough to witness Bowie and
the Sex Pistols – who left a boomeresque imprint on Britain with New
Labour'.[2] This was the generation that most dramatically changed
Britain's social mores. It was during the heyday of this generation that
the music press was writing in the 1990s.

This generation had grown up in the shadow of Psychedelia and
Woodstock, anti-Vietnam protests and free love, and always admired
and esteemed those things associated with modern American society.
By contrast, Britain remained more petty-minded and fuddy-duddy.
Well into the 1970s and 1980s, it was a place more akin to Mary
Whitehouse than Janis Joplin. In 1985 Harold Macmillan had crit-
icized Margaret Thatcher for 'selling off the family silver'; a man
and a phrase reminiscent of the old gentry that America never had
and which still held sway to some extent until it finally withered
in the following decade. 'Cool Brittania' sought to undo all this,
to challenge the remaining social hierarchies and mores that had
not been disrupted nearly enough by the largely America-dominated
1960s radicalism. New Labour's boldest aim was to make Britain a
cosmopolitan liberal state, globalized in its economy, meritocratic in
outlook, shorn of the privileges of yesteryear.

The British late-Boomers look to 1960s America as their year zero.
This intention took shape at the level of popular culture by presenting
a liberal, cosmopolitan identity for the British as normative, highlighting the Britain of the 1960s as being as seminal for Britain as the
USA, though had not been as seminal as New Labour apparatchiks
might have hoped. People in their thirties and forties in the 1990s,
born in the late 1960s and the 1970s, thus sought to show how the
Britain of the 1960s was not merely derivative from American culture,
but something important and significant in its own right. This conviction is certainly true to some extent when it comes to the British
popular music of the 1960s. So it was that these British late-Boomers

should be associated with what was the dominant fixation of the music press in the mid 1990s, called 'Britpop'.

Britpop originally referred to a group of bands that celebrated the allegedly non-derivative Britishness of their music, imitating the Beatles, the Rolling Stones, the Who, the Small Faces, and so on. The bands most enamoured of the music press were presented as revelling in their 'Britishness'. Photo shoots for magazine covers invariably had Union Jacks and Austin Minis in the background. England football shirts and cans of lager were common, supposedly as an 'up yours' to the old gentility of Harold Macmillan's generation. But the affected celebration of working-class identity was not really convincing. Bands like Blur aped what were genuinely cockney bands in the 1960s. The East End of London by the 1990s was nothing like it had been then. The ethnic make-up of the city had already changed significantly enough to mean the rag-and-bone men, the flat-cap-wearing market traders and the rituals of the dog-races were already vanishing historical curiosities. Britpoppers had an outdated and idealized caricature of urban working-class life. This caricature was attractive to the wealthier suburbs and meant nothing in the inner city. It was at this time that the term 'mockney' entered the language, meaning one who imitated a genuine cockney in an unconvincing way.

Seeking to define something on the basis of what it is not merely reflects the contrasted thing all the more vividly. For all the faux-British posturing of the Britpoppers, they had adopted an American narrative and just put it in a flat cap and an England shirt. The indelibility of 1960s America still dominated the narrative: challenging the privileges of an old imperial order, celebrating newly minted human rights and social liberalism, thinking and acting globally, treating local concerns as disdainfully petty-minded, the family as outdated tribalism. The Britpoppers tried concertedly not to be derivative, but ended up inescapably imitative as a result.

This pattern applies to the music that actually did come from the inner London of the 1990s, when it broke into the music press. The Britpoppers took interest in it because they felt it was not derivative: a 'British form of black music!' Hip-hop was important for late-Boomers in the states. As Christopher Caldwell points out, they were a generation for whom Sugar Hill Gang's 'Rappers Delight' became a hit 'just as the first post-Boomers entered high school and imposed itself on an [American] national radio audience with Grandmaster Flash's *The Message* (1982) just as they were heading off to college'.[3] 'This is our hip-hop', the Britpoppers would say, narrativizing the scene according to the American paradigm. They imposed a set of categories from elsewhere.

Movements of black music from the States are completely inextricable from their African American character. The importance of the phrase 'black music' for the States cannot be divorced from the specific trajectory of American race-relations. Theorists had long since asked whether the complexity of jazz bears some traces of syncopated African drumming and highlighted how Blues gives voice to the misery and injustice suffered by African Americans at the hands of their oppressors. The inextricability of race-relations and hip-hop is such that it cannot be overstated. Therefore, it is reasonable to ask if presenting the early 1990s music of London as 'our black music' can really hold for a country with a different trajectory of race-relations. This suggestion leads us straight into very contentious territory.

It might be better not even to touch on it, to let it slumber and be forgotten like the old record shops, similarly kept in a back room or basement quarters where the unwary passers-by on the high street need not be disturbed by what it suggests. Maybe it needs to be contained, like the soundproofing of those old rooms, and passed by into even greater obscurity than the habits of respect such rooms engendered. Before even being elucidated, the suggestion invites accusations of wanting to pretend British history does not have shamefully racist incidents in its past. One might equally be accused of wanting to pretend there is no problem with racial disparities in British society today, no challenges when it comes to fair policing and education.

But there is no reason why these accusations need be unleashed and no reason why asking this question entails downplaying or denying the issues at stake. It is just to ask if there is a distinct trajectory, including injustices and sufferings yes, but a different trajectory all the same. It is merely to ask whether relations between black and white Americans can be superimposed onto relations between black and white citizens of Britain and remain genuinely representative and accurate.

Let us imagine what a contemporary commentator on race, forged on the American model, would make of the scenario of those early 1990s record shops just described. To say race just didn't seem that important at the time, that it was noticeable but not particularly significant, would be deemed hugely problematic. It is, sin of all sins, it is the claim to have been 'colourblind'. Today's dominant narrative dictates that any projecting of contexts or situations as 'un-racialized' are the most racist projections of all, because only those privileged enough to share the identity of the dominant race could be so entitled. This is a key tenet of theorists like Kimberlé Crenshaw, who argued for 'the social significance of identity categories'.[4] 'Whiteness' is presented by the dominant mindset as 'the absence of racial identity'.[5] Pushed further, this reaches a point like that mentioned in the previous chapter, undoing our commonality *as* human. Human nature is racialized, because there is no dimension to one's self that can be extricated from it. Crenshaw writes that it is wrong for black people to say or think 'I am a person who happens to be Black', because this is 'straining for a certain universality' and 'a concomitant dismissal of the imposed category ("Black") as contingent, circumstantial, non-determinate'. To say 'I am Black', by contrast, 'takes the socially imposed identity and empowers it as an anchor of subjectivity', making it a 'positive discourse of self-identification'.[6]

Jean-Paul Sartre said that 'anti-racist racism is the only road that will lead to the abolition of racial differences'.[7] If he is right, it feels there is a long way until we reach that destination. Whether or not the ownership of what theorists like Crenshaw define as 'Blackness' is liberating and empowering for African American contexts is not at issue here. The point is that, as 'socially imposed', this concept must differ in meaning in different societies, for the different cultures that impose it and for black people of different cultures, who may each interpret the word differently. Thomas Chatterton Williams says 'we all make, according to our own geographical and cultural orientations, inferences about other people and ourselves based on the loose interplay of physical traits, language, custom and rationality, all of which lack any fixed or universal meaning'.[8] These things thus differ in different contexts. They will differ in settings where black and white people have lived alongside each other in different times and places to the USA of today. It is no coincidence that the example of early 1990s London includes the intermingling of mostly Afro-Caribbean and white working-class people. These kids were the kids of those who had lived alongside each other for a couple of generations. These were kids who had, to some extent, inherited organically and naturally fusing cultures. Yet experiences like this are not used as helpful resources for approaching issues with immigration and racial tensions; people do not ask whether, or how, different cultures can interact and fuse.

Again, this is not to say there aren't grave problems of injustice in the history of the Windrush Generation's experience of the UK. Nor is 'colourblindness' actually the best way to describe those record shops in any case. It is not that people did not see or register colour at all. It is rather that racial designation or categorization was not the starting-point of all encounters, not something people were admonished to hold before their minds in each moment. There were person-to-person encounters between people on the basis of a shared culture. That these encounters happened often between people of different races, without that difference seeming particularly important, reminds us of the ancient understanding of 'culture' as that which cultivates and edifies human nature. People had formed 'habits of respect', even if only partially applicable to certain areas of life. These 'habits of respect' were ignored after the scene was racialized by well-meaning white people who had studied people like Crenshaw and wanted to signal their virtuous status. Sartre says 'anti-racist racism' is the only road to the abolition of racial differences. But there is another road and that road is culture.

Heightened racial categorization as a means of achieving mutual respect between peoples functions differently to culturally formed habits of respect. One is artificial and imposed, the other organic and participatory. One holds that even human nature is racialized, the other that habits become 'second natures'. Then our natures develop precisely through ongoing shared endeavour within the same society.

The direction of travel is away from racial categorization and into a shared and distinctive culture. This does not imitate histories from elsewhere. It takes the manifold derivations at play in the present and allows a new coherence to emerge. You have to earn the ability to hear this coherence, however. At first it seems chaotic and impossible to make out among the din. Well-meaning people from the suburbs then try to engineer coherence by using racial categorization as a means to engender respect.

Well-meaning (and well-to-do) experts try to inculcate respect among people through the lever of racialization. Those record shops are a long way from the Unconscious Bias training sessions of today. Yet the effects of transposing American forms of racial etiquette onto other contexts feels at worst like the shoddiest examples of that early 1990s music. Experiences are forced into a mould that does not fit, intentions restrained to the point of mutilation. A wealthy white person, from an exclusively white part of the country, tells you how to interact with people of other races without causing offence. You are admonished to register immediately when in the company of a person of colour and hold that thought before your mind so you can minimize the influence of white supremacy on your behaviour.

At such a session I found out I am married to someone who, according to the definition being used, is herself a person of colour, because she's Middle Eastern. Discussing this later that evening, she was bemused. I also learned that relationships between a person of colour and a white person are particularly difficult, because of the mismatched levels of power and privilege between the two parties. We laughed at how ill-fitting these categorizations are for two people who grew up in London. They didn't apply to real life, to the real habits of respect that form between people over the years.

The new etiquette is not built by daily 'living among' different races, it is learned through peer-reviewed journals and PowerPoint slides. The new etiquette is not formed from below the surface of consciousness by the interpenetration of cultural influences in a specific place. It seeks consciously to reprogramme the unconscious, the place where culture takes root. Culture is then not a source of unity, but a dangerous place steeped only in prejudice and hatred on the one hand, fear and suffering on the other. Then it is not about fellow citizenship, but about either people as always either only recipients of racial privilege or victims of injustice. But this distinction is not a genuine binary. The binary has been broken. There is no boundary between behaviours deemed racist and those not racist. There was once a boundary marked by behaviours like slurs, jokes, acts of violence or instances of preferential treatment. Now it is a spectrum of degrees of racism only, in which everyone shares.

Language of 'allies' and 'allyship' is intrinsically linked to this broken binary. It is inconceivable, in the new paradigm, for someone not to have thought much about racial injustice and not to be considered racist. Racism pervades everything, there is no boundary with non-racism anymore. People have to be situated on the spectrum of degrees of racism and 'allyship' defines the positive end of that spectrum for the privileged. Everyone must then participate and be conscripted into the scheme. Not to be an ally is to be unashamedly racist. Allyship means neutrality is not an option. No one can be apolitical or just focused on other things.

There is another important dimension to the use of this term, which breaks with its earlier meanings. To be an ally is not quite allyship in a common cause, as such. Or rather, it is allyship in a cause that is not held in common, strictly speaking. It is to be ally with the cause of addressing injustice for those who fall victim to it. This is the pressing concern, of course, but for long-term social coherence another side is necessary too. This other side involves the fact that those deemed privileged can also be deeply invested in achieving racial coherence and unity, for the wellbeing of the good of their own society, not only by forsaking its injustices. With both sides at play, there is a truly common cause.

The artificial and superimposed approach tackles problems primarily through legal means and through the grievance or complaint procedures of HR departments. Christopher Caldwell points out that, to some extent, this makes sense in an American context. Because the States did not have a 'shared heritage', all 'the eggs of national cohesion are placed in the basket of the constitution'.[9] Constitutional law is then a lever of racial cohesion, leading to federally led legal initiatives like Affirmative Action, racial quotas for universities, diversity regulations in the corporate sector. Caldwell says this 'top-down management of various ethnic, regional and social groups' had 'always been the task of empires'.[10] This is ironic, as the American constitution is the loudest rebuke against the imperial world. Imperialism meant imposing one set of norms upon another, holding one set of norms as culturally superior, pressing forward with a one-size-fits-all approach to everything.

Elizabeth Lasch-Quinn argues that 'sensitivity training' and 'racial etiquette' actually invert the original intentions of the Civil Rights movement.[11] As Chatterton Williams states, we don't 'interact with groups or structures, but with people'. Remembering this, he suggests, might allow people to be 'free enough to decide' against 'passively' or 'even just uncritically' reproducing 'their racial designations'.[12] A critique of categorization need not be a call for colourblindness. It should rather be like Chatterton Williams' suggestion that we strive 'to develop a vision of ourselves strong and supple enough both to acknowledge the lingering importance of group identities, while also attenuating, rather than reinforcing, the extent to which such identities are able to define us'.[13] It is a call to let a new coherence emerge within a shared culture, not to force-grow a coherence by categories transposed from elsewhere. It is not colourblind because it celebrates that which is derivative. But through habits of respect a new coherence can emerge on its own terms. Our ears have only to adjust to the confluence. Then something new can be free to take flight.

7

Responsibility

The light of the old independent record shops of London had its own distinctive hue or, rather, a distinctive blend of hues, in and by which a new coherence took flight through shared habits. By contrast, the stiltedness of acute-conscious awareness of racial categories as a professionalized etiquette restrains the exploratory character of human interaction and relationships. Sadly, the media commentators on that scene missed some genuinely interesting and important things about it as they categorized it with exclusively racial terms. That is, something was emerging that was distinctive. It was Epicurean. These were habits of respect forged through enjoyment and pleasure. It was a subculture based on feeling good, on music, dancing, all manner of emotional and physical pleasure.

But the light that settled in London and shone in this way settled differently elsewhere, a couple of years later. Out in the countryside of the south west of England, particularly, it was morphing in different ways again. Away from the clubs of London, young people were taking sounds systems out into the wilds and holding parties in forests, on moors, plains and farmland. The music developed in ways to match these surroundings. There were fewer samples, little or no voices. It was deliberately in- or non-human. Tunes seemed to go on forever, endlessly looping the same sound and making only small tweaks and adjustments to it that only an initiate would recognize and respond to. These parties out in the countryside developed a sensibility of their own, connected to the burgeoning environmental movement. Around the parties formed tribes of nomadic, technologically astute, travelling circuses. These brought sound systems and performers in convoys across the land. Some people attended these parties and decided never to go home; they ran away to join the circus.

Around the same time, this environmental movement was engaging in high-profile battles with the government's large-scale road-building scheme. There had been battles around the demolition of houses to make way for the M11 link road in east London. An extension to the M3 cutting through the countryside of Twyford Down in Hampshire involved protests and evictions that made the national press. The biggest and most long-running of these road protests took place on land to the north-west of the town of Newbury in West Berkshire. To the south-east of this town was Greenham Common, to the north-west, Snelsmore Common. As the place of intersections between north–south and east–west, roads in the town were gridlocked. A bypass constructed years previously was now surrounded by urban sprawl and used by local residents going about town as well as heavy-goods lorries and long-distance drivers. So a new bypass had been planned to run west of the town, far outcircling its north-western perimeter and thereby cutting through Snelsmore Common.

Snelsmore is a site of special scientific interest. It is mostly wild woods and also has open plains of heathland with gorse and lavender growing on them. There are chalk grasslands dotted around the edges and some deep marshland in the centre. Various little streams and ponds can be found among the trees. With the tension around road protests having built over the preceding years, this protest was billed as presenting the opportunity for the flagship battle. On sites along the proposed route, the art of 'tree hugging' had now developed into a set of clearly defined tactics. People now built networks of intersecting wooden shelters in the highest branches of neighbouring trees, making it extremely difficult for workmen to set to work with their chainsaws. They were developing a new tactic of underground tunnelling, creating criss-crossed burrows and small chambers under the earth, which meant heavy machinery could enter the woods without causing the ground to collapse. The 'Battle of Newbury' ran from the summer of 1995 to the spring months of 1996. It mostly centred on flashpoints when security guards and bailiffs were coached out to Snelsmore with police alongside, to drag the protestors out of the trees and coax them out of the tunnels. Early morning evictions made the following day's national news regularly for a few months. Reporters filmed triumphant workmen as they set to work with their chainsaws, having just cleared a few square metres of an encampment at dawn.

The travelling sound systems appeared at various sites along the route at certain times, holding parties at which protestors and local youths gathered. The music scene corresponding to the protest network was not Epicurean, however, but more Schopenhaurian. If one were to theorize this element of the subculture, it was about music making contact with unseen forces. These were the forces of nature, from which, it was said, modern civilization was alienated and ruptured. Making contact with them again would empower people to take proper responsibility for the natural world. This responsibility would be forged by human technology meeting the natural world in electronic music, giving the natural world a voice and expression it could not otherwise attain. The endless hypnotic rhythm was said to be symbolic of the turning of the Earth on its axis, the rhythmic rising of the moon and the sun, the turning of the seasons. The peaks and drops in intensity of the sounds were said to symbolize the flowering, harvesting and decay of the plants and trees of the Earth. The legends of people attending such parties and never going home built a corresponding mythos around them, connected to the Levellers, to ancient tales of youths living nomadically among the trees and in the earth like Robin Hood and his Merry Men, or of the fairytales of old, where people eat a forbidden fruit and vanish from the normal plain of existence immediately.

One sound system released an album with a mission statement for this techno-meets-nature Schopenhaurianism on its back cover:

> It is our mission to discover the ever-changing horizons, to continually re-establish new parameters and to explore and secure each new level as we find it. It is our purpose to destroy the inertia that has been responsible for the demise of the lifeforce on our planet. It is our aim to positively motivate the people and the nation. It's time to wake the planet up.

The reality, as ever, was far less romantic. How much of the account just given is truth or fantasy remains unexamined. The locals saw the incomers as privileged, middle-class dropouts, just students camping out for a few days between lectures at the nearby universities of Oxford or Winchester or Reading. Like at Greenham, there were scuffles and battles between locals and the incomers, who were termed 'stinkweeds' by punters in the town-centre pubs. The local press were unsympathetic towards them, yet the *Guardian* was rapturous with praise. Local people wanted the heavy traffic out of their town. They wanted short-distance drives not to take hours. They wanted not to struggle with bags of shopping because they couldn't drive to the supermarket. They wanted roads to be safer for pedestrians, the town centre not to be so noisy and full of engine fumes.

The MP of the town had the difficult task of wanting to seem to be taking environmental concerns seriously, while at the same representing constituents for whom there was near unanimous support for the bypass. One way of doing this was to highlight that the environment of the town itself was bring destroyed by the heavy traffic. Air quality was a particular concern for the local population and it would be improved for routing the traffic out of town.

Now, it might be thought that the protestors would respond to this concern by saying there is little to be gained by improving air quality for one community, while destroying it for the flora, fauna, birds and animals five miles out to the west. It might seem even more likely that they would point out that carbon dioxide would still be released into the atmosphere on the new bypass, causing detrimental effects to planetary wellbeing even if not choking the lungs of the children in town. Interestingly, however, this move to planetary responsibility was not the most natural response back then. This is seen in an exchange between the local MP David Rendel and the *Guardian* journalist George Monbiot, who is now a high-profile voice of the planetary 'climate emergency'. With a view to the air quality argument, Rendel said to Monbiot during a demonstration on Snelsmore Common in 1995:

> If I may say so, a lot of the facts produced by the protestors have been themselves very much misleading . . . the bypass will bring

environmental benefits greatly bigger than the environmental disadvantages.

Monbiot responded:

> You call environmental benefits trashing three sites of Special Scientific Interest, one mesiolithic archeological site, one Roman site, a civil war battlefield? These are irreplaceable parts of our national heritage. Without these we lose our sense of belonging, our sense of self, our sense of nationhood. What you are doing here is tearing apart the fabric of the nation, which helps us to be whole people, which helps us to be people who feel we have a place. This is a crime that will be remembered for generations.

Such sentiments from George Monbiot are surprising. Around ten years later he wrote a riposte to colleagues at the *Guardian* who had called for a renovation of patriotism and a sense of national identity to counter the threat of homegrown jihadism after the London Bombings. Tristram Hunt had called for there to be pride in 'British values' and he was supported by Jonathan Friedland, who highlighted the values of 'political liberalism and intellectual inquiry'. Monbiot responded by arguing that prioritizing the British role in these things was 'chauvinism'. He wrote: 'Britain also has an appalling record of imperialism and pig-headed jingoism and, when you wave the flag, no one can be sure which record you are celebrating.'

On the question of British history, Monbiot also took issue with the *Daily Telegraph*'s listing of '10 core values of the British identity', whose adoption would be said to help 'prevent another terrorist attack'. Among them was 'history' ('British children inherit . . . a stupendous series of national achievements'). For Monbiot, this celebration of history was just a repetition of the errors of the jihadis. He said it meant just replacing 'an Islamic vision of history' with 'an Etonian one'.[1] By the time of the Brexit vote in 2016, Monbiot was arguing that the UK does not have 'a strong cultural sense of nationhood' at all, for 'every cultural reference point is poorly defined, weak and contested'. 'National pride', he said, is now 'toxic'.[2,3]

A few years previously, the same journalist was unabashed at pointing out that the natural landscape included 'irreplaceable parts of our national heritage' without which 'we lose our sense of belonging, our sense of self, our sense of nationhood'. To destroy the natural landscape would, therefore, tear apart 'the fabric of the nation, which helps us to be whole people, which helps us to be people who feel we have a place'. It is important not to overstate the case here. Monbiot is not necessarily contradicting himself, strictly speaking. Holding to the importance of belonging, of feeling 'we have a place', could be separable from the chauvinism about 'values' he later railed against. Nonetheless it is curious he could once have celebrated national belonging as regards ancient history and landscape, but does not so much as mention this when he condemns national belonging as regards more recent historical and social contexts. It seems as if his response in 1995 could perhaps not be made now, for now the discussion must move to global, transnational concerns, away from local and national stewardship of culture. But in this stewardship, environmental and social responsibilities were seen as linked.

At a party on one of the protest sites in the woods of Snelsmore in early 1996, the tale of a recent event was eagerly told and retold. On hearing it for the first time, it seemed one of those silly tales that tree-hugging hippies, probably under the influence of magic mushrooms, would tell each other with laughable solemnity. There had been a showdown earlier that week around a cluster of oak trees. The showdown followed the usual sequence of events at first. Protestors were removed from the trees by bailiffs at the first light of dawn. The workmen set to work with their chainsaws. The protestors looked on in disarray, watched over by a couple of mounted police. But then, something different to the normal run of things happened. Two horses appeared in the distance, running concertedly down the grassland of a nearby hill, making their way across the paddocks in the foreground. They eventually reached the people gathered around the workmen revving their chainsaws at the foot of the old oaks. The sun was still rising, the morning mist was rolling over the grass and fields. The bailiffs and protestors were tired. Both groups rubbed their eyes in disbelief. The nearer the horses got to the oaks, the more keenly those present scanned the horizon to look for some riders or stable-keepers in the distance, so they could know where these majestic creatures came from.

When the horses reached the crowd, they had no saddles or bridles or bits. They seemed to be wild horses that had just galloped out of the woods. They hadn't been put off by the deafening chainsaws, they had run directly to the oaks where people were gathered. After the horses arrived, the workmen tried to start up their work again, but the horses ran to and fro around them, neighing and whinnying. The workmen kept starting and stopping uneasily, worried at what the horses might do next. One of the horses then tried to engage a police stallion, going up on his rear legs. The stallion backed away in fear, while the officer in the saddle did her best to keep him calm.

The protestors rushed back to the base camp to tell everyone about what had happened. The tale was embellished as it passed along the shanty-town settlements in the trees. Some said the horses had caused a workman to drop his chainsaw and run away into the forest, others that the police stallion was kicked to the floor and the officer sent tumbling to the ground. There were reports that some of the bailiffs were so spooked they never returned to work on Snelsmore Common again.

The protestors said these were ancient wild horses, who had been grazing incognito in this countryside for centuries. The tree-huggers living in the woods had seen herds of these horses gathered in the clearings between the trees where thick bracken, ferns and grasses flourished. Not only were there herds of such horses, the protestors said, but these horses had some sort of telepathic link with the protestors. The protestors felt as if the horses knew and understood why they were there, that they saw them as fellow-travellers fighting the evil forces coming to destroy their homeland.

Fantastical stories abounded, of the tree-people being guided by the horses through the woodland and shown where they should set up camp, of their being shown bubbling brooks with water so clean they could drink it from the ground, and to remote sunlit pools where people could bathe and wash. They thought neglected means of communication between the human mind and the natural world were being opened up again. This was a symbiosis and interconnection between the natural and human worlds, which had long since been blocked-off by the lifestyles of modern civilization. By returning to living among the trees, surviving at subsistence level through foraging among nature, these means of communication were being re-opened. People said they had seen Puck dancing among the bluebells and strange, shiningly tall elf-like figures flitting between the tree-trunks with echoing laughter. The horses were said to be spirit guides, mediating between the faery and human settlements in the woods, building alliances between the material and astral worlds, to defend the ancient trees.

It was self-evident to the tree-people that those wild horses came to disrupt the felling of that cluster of oaks. They must have done so because they particularly loved those old trees. Maybe they sheltered there regularly after grazing on the nearby land. Maybe they had memories of seeking shelter under them when they were foals. Or maybe they sensed the dereliction of the protestors watching the trees being felled, they heard their mourning carried as whispers by the shining elves that fly across the tumbling mist as it settles in dreamy pools in the fields. Then the horses left their stations in the forest and rushed through the bracken to come to their aid.

* * *

Absurd as all this is, years later a video of the event appeared online. Insofar as the video is to be believed, it shows two apparently wild ponies (not horses) appearing from the surrounding countryside during the tree-felling and causing a kerfuffle. The most likely reason for their appearance is anxiety and fear caused by the noise. Although they certainly look wild, it is curious that they approach the crowd so boldly. They must have been at least partially domesticated and at ease with human contact. They appear quite young, perhaps adolescents who broke away from their herd out of curiosity and excitement having been attracted by the scent of the police horses on their patch.

The scene is thus believable without accepting the fantastical tales that were connected with it among the tree-people. There is still an unanswered question, however, about where these ponies came from. There are moors and woodlands in southern England where wild ponies still graze, the New Forest in Hampshire and Exmoor in Devon. But Exmoor is nearly 150 miles from Snelsmore Common, the New Forest over fifty. If the protestors' claims that herds of equines were occasionally seen around this countryside were to be believed, these two ponies could not simply be explained away as escapees from a local stables.

Everything falls into place when it is learned that, just a couple of years before the bypass battle had begun, a scheme had been launched whereby small herds of both Exmoor and New Forest ponies were introduced to Snelsmore Common for reasons of 'conservation grazing'. This is a way of controlling and limiting the growth of more aggressive plants, without using the blunt instruments of human tech- nology, such as weedkillers or strimmers, which kill everything else in the vicinity of the plants they seek to remove. Aggressive, non-native plants that threaten the local ecosystem are thus controlled without doing even more damage. The scheme had been successful and the herds are still there to this day, reproducing and replenishing them- selves in their West Berkshire setting.

At once, a cynic can now laugh at the absurdity of the hippies, who were convinced some ancient inhabitants of this land and its trees were joining forces with them, who, aided by magic mushrooms, were convinced magical dimensions of human and natural communication were being opened up once again. 'It is our mission to discover the ever-changing horizons', but there was no faerieland between the nat- ural and the human worlds after all.

A poem accompanies the video of the wild ponies disrupting the tree-felling. It begins:

> The English oak, its majesty once revered,
> now seen as an obstacle needing to be cleared,
> the respect it once commanded has disappeared,
> along with the respect and pride its homeland once enjoyed
> England – what has become of you?

These wild horses were, the poet says, 'An Omen – and echo from the past'. The poet actually has a point. This echoing past is not faerieland, however. There is a realm mediating between the natural and the human and this is the realm from whence Puck and all the elves and wood sprites of English folklore derive: culture. As with Monbiot's answer to the local MP, people could, back then, speak of defending the natural environment as a defence of culture, and vice versa. This was a time before localized culture was deemed toxic by those same people with environmental concerns. This was when there was a straightforward instinct, a sense of allegiance that included even the land, for 'our sense of belonging, our sense of self, our sense of nationhood'.

The English oak is an echo from the past, an echo that reverberates through culture. It has a cultural history that is not replaced by a reforesting scheme to offset carbon emissions. It is emblematic of England, used for naval warships, making up the timbers in Tudor buildings, enshrined in mythology and legend from even pre-Christian times. These are echoes today's environmentalists can no longer hear, yet the poem suggests they were once heard loud and clear by the road protestors. The very fact the wild ponies were living in the woods is in fact cultural. They had been introduced to the countryside by conservationists. They were there because human culture, the conservation movement, had put them there. They were not simply 'wild', that is, purely natural. Nor were they simply 'domestic', connected only to human activity. They did, in this sense, mediate between two worlds of nature and humanity and through the intermediate realm of culture.

In an age deemed 'ecological', continuities between the natural and the human world are resurfacing because the impact of the latter on the former is so topical. Bruno Latour's *We Have Never Been Modern* posits the view that any 'fundamental dichotomy between nature and culture' is a product of the Enlightenment, presumably because the advent of natural science and the inductive method rendered the natural as a meaningless mass of relatively inert matter.[4] If culture reflects nature and cultures form human lives we are much closer to nature than we think. From the natural side, Nathan Lyons' *Signs in the Dust* discusses at length the phenomenon of 'biosemiotics', where non-human organisms employ signs for communication, something once considered exclusive to humans, the core activity of culture.[5] There are therefore rudimentary forms of culture in the non-human world. Peter Wohlleben's *The Hidden Life of Trees: What they Feel, How they Communicate – Discoveries from a Secret World* outlines the ways trees pass messages to each other in ancient woodlands.[6]

A human–nature porosity is also present whenever human cultural expressions are marked by natural conditions. There is a long history of climate, particularly, having profound effects on human character. It is mentioned tangentially in Hippocrates and much later in Jean Bodin's *Methodius*. Nikolaus Pevsner suggests that the Abbé Dubos in 1719 was the first to apply this connection between climate and character to the arts, before the same impulse was taken up with gusto by Johann Joachim Winckelmann for 'his interpretation of Greek art'. From thence, says Pevsner, it made its way into the Romantics.[7] It then contributes to the struggle against the senselessness of nature revealed by the Enlightenment.

Peter Ackroyd's *Albion: The Origins of the English Imagination* situates the origin of an English sensibility in the land of England itself. Whereas typical Enlightenment and post-Enlightenment genealogies of English culture tended to begin with the early modern period, Ackroyd claims there are continuities in cultural character going back at least as far as Beowulf. Such continuities must, he says, find their roots in the natural world of England as the one point of continuity throughout all the social change between then and now. He says that 'a native spirit persists though time and circumstance, all the more powerful for being generally unacknowledged' and this spirit originates in the land and not in the country's people.[8]

Albion was published in 2004, while England was going through dramatic demographic change. ONS records show that, between 1964 and 1997, numbers of migrants were in the tens of thousands, but from 1998 it has remained consistently in hundreds of thousands, peaking at 323,000 in 2015. Concerns of continuity, of cultural stewardship, were therefore growing in the popular mind and *Albion*'s publication happened just before an unprecedented movement of people from former Eastern Bloc countries to the UK in 2005. This was a time before Eurosceptic views posed any serious electoral threat, long before the 2016 referendum. It was still just about socially acceptable to raise questions about the stewardship and preservation of a cultural tradition undergoing dramatic rises in incoming migration, without being condemned as xenophobic or racist.

Ackroyd offered an attractive way to do it. His approach could maintain a proud sense of cultural heritage and intellectual tradition, without making any accommodation whatsoever to ethnicity. Indeed, he was explicit about the fact the English cultural tradition has long since been multi-racial, saying it had a 'mixed and mongrel style', which is 'hybrid like the people from which it derives, but is distinctive precisely because of its willingness to adopt other influences'.[9] In this he was inspired by Sir Philip Sidney calling the English style of drama a 'mungrell' style and he employs this term to 'the English intelligence' itself.[10] Ackroyd here offered a way to celebrate immigration as a social good, while simultaneously celebrating cultural identity and continuity. One fed constructively into the other.

More recently, Robert Winder's *The Last Wolf: The Hidden Springs of Englishness* draws similar conclusions. He also works from natural conditions like climate to posit an English character of mind, a character that cannot be ethnically constituted, for this is 'an Anglo-Saxon–Viking–Celtic witch's brew of an island governed by Norman occupiers'.[11] Some might want to make recourse to DNA data and suchlike to question whether England was really so multi-racial. A more convincing response comes from Paul Embery, who says the idea of 'a nation of immigrants' is 'probably calculatedly – misleading'. He says it 'ignores the dramatic disparities in the scale and pace of immigration throughout the ages, particularly the fact that the level of intensity of immigration into Britain over the past twenty or so years is of an utterly different magnitude to that which was experienced before then'.[12] Embery goes on write that 'the more diverse a society, the weaker the sense of social solidarity among citizens is likely to be'. So, 'social and cultural distinctions between citizens can be, and often are, gravely problematic in marshalling concern for shared concerns and difficulties'.[13]

Embery is convincing, at least in view of recent volumes of immigration. By Ackroyd's reckoning, we can let the land express itself through whomever might live upon it, for this is what the land has always done. But this process of land (nature) speaking through people (culture) worked differently when people depended on their climate for their food and livelihood, when natural conditions defined all elements of human experience. In a technologized world, people can adopt exactly the same lifestyle in either Singapore or Streatham, in Timbuctoo or Teesside. Moreover, building on Embery's criticisms about considering diversity an unalloyed good in all circumstances, surely the most effective way for widespread concern for the environment to impact behaviour is for that concern to lead naturally out of the sources of cohesion and belonging, out of local cultures. The old instincts shown by Monbiot and the poet who wrote about the wild ponies thus have much sense in them. When our sense of place and belonging is threatened, that is when people will defend the land.

By sharp contrast, today's environmentalism goes straight to the global, planetary scenario. Today's most well-known environmental movement, Extinction Rebellion, was founded after thirty years of failed attempts at transnational, global negotiations to reduce carbon emissions. But the organization responded to this global failure with the threat of all-encompassingly global scenarios. They adopt the language of war and crisis, speaking of 'ecogenocide' and human extinction. For most people, these are concepts to which it is extremely difficult to relate. Compared to what planning enthusiasts called 'NIMBYism' and 'Little Englandism', there is no question of what garners the more popular support.

Moreover, words like 'extinction' and 'genocide', however real these threats might be, push the debate to a fanatical extreme where the choice is between obedience or death. There is a pointedly anti-freedom strain to those who speak of a 'climate emergency'. They specialize in blocking traffic and forcing shared public spaces into gridlock, making shops, bridges, offices and pubs close. Old-school environmentalists have complained about the controlling, passive aggressive bans XR place on drinking cans of beers at their events.

The movement deliberately seeks out mass incarceration as its primary tactic. George Monbiot said at an XR rally in 2018, 'The only time when people know it's serious is when people are prepared to sacrifice their liberty.' He didn't acknowledge that voluntary arrest is nearly always the preserve of the materially privileged.

During the Covid lockdowns of 2020 and 2021, there was a spate of social media posts showing improved carbon dioxide levels with the comment 'nature is healing'. This was a wonderful thing no doubt, but it led people to wonder if 'climate lockdowns' could be a feature of years to come, this time with graphs where the curve of upward CO_2 levels had to be flattened, rather than deaths in the ICU. Indeed, George Monbiot appeared on TV and radio arguing that lockdowns should become an invaluable tool in offsetting the climate crisis in future.

Greta Thunberg described XR's justification for direct action by saying, 'We can't save the world by playing by the rules, because rules have to be changed. Everything needs to change. And it has to start today.' Is 'changing all the rules' really the best way forward? Maybe tried and tested means of obedience might avoid, not just death and imminent doom, but all this anti-freedom sentiment too. The idea that one set of problems can be tackled by ignoring or rewriting the experience of life elsewhere does not ring true. Rules are sediments of experience, a deposit left by lives before our own. Conservation of cultures can therefore lead into the conservation of environments and vice versa. It is not then about losing freedom to avoid ecogenocide, so much as becoming more free to enjoy and appreciate the natural world among which particular communities live.

What is deemed obedient through time in culture can thus lead to freedom. Conservation and conservatism are intrinsically related and precisely those things cherished by social conservatives contain the necessary resources for environmental conservation. Social liberalism, by contrast, is inconsistent and incoherent, seeking to forsake all limits under the rubric of voluntary choice and then being left with totalitarian responses to limit those choices when they threaten the existence of the whole. The word 'traditional' is celebrated by liberals when used for farming, forestry or means of irrigation. The same word is considered irredeemably toxic when applied to gender roles, families or religious beliefs.

Tradition is the same thing in both applications, the same when used of people or places, culture or nature. It bespeaks the tried and tested ways to bring the best out of life, while causing the minimum of damage and the fewest deleterious long-term effects. Tradition fosters community between people just as it fosters community with nature. Wendell Berry points out that 'community . . . aspires towards stability', it 'strives to balance change with constancy'. This is why, for Berry, 'community life places such high value on neighbourly love, marital fidelity, local loyalty, the integrity and continuity of family life, respect for the old and instruction of the young'. A 'vital community' like this 'draws its life, so far as possible, from local sources'.[14]

Roger Scruton's *Green Philosophy* is the fullest exposition of the natural proclivity that should exist between social and environmental conservation. He writes that 'conservatism and conservation are two aspects of a single long-term policy, which is that of husbanding resources and ensuring their renewal'. He lists resources as both 'social', meaning what is 'embodied in laws, customs and institutions', and also 'material', what is 'contained in the environment'.[15] Conservatism is described as inherently local, emphasizing 'historical loyalties' and 'local affections'. Liberalism is an ideology that is inherently 'global' and so cannot see how cultures include 'homeostatic systems' just like those of the natural world, meaning 'traditions, customs and the common law', 'families' and 'civil associations'.[16]

Revivifying such systems should be generative of freedom. This is the freedom granted by social cohesion, by self-maintaining and stable communities. Systems with analogous properties pertain in the natural world, so the virtues gleaned in conserving one should bear fruit in conserving the other. The alternative is a fight between two forms of globalism. The first is globalized capital, which pushes for unlimited growth and ever-greater acquisition of wealth by making use of whatever resources can be acquired most cheaply across the globe. The second is globalized culture, which attacks the notion of continuity between the human and the natural at the root by not valuing the rootedness of particular people in particular places, considering such rootedness as intrinsically toxic.

Global responsibility can only offer either forced obedience or certain death. It seeks ever 'new parameters' to 'reset' or 'wake the planet up'. Local responsibility bespeaks a porosity between local communities and local environments. This responsibility offers an organic mode of obedience, rooted in tradition, which flowers and bears fruit in a life-giving freedom, not in freedom's destruction under the fear of death.

8

Discipline

Before boarding an airliner bound for Munich on 29 September 1938, Neville Chamberlain declared, 'When I come back, I hope I may be able to say as Hotspur says in *Henry IV*: "Out of this nettle, danger, we pluck this flower, safety."' Just under a year later, Britain declared war on Germany. Chamberlain's quoting of Shakespeare in the midst of a diplomatic crisis appears haplessly inept. Its naivety fits the image of him going to broker a gentleman's agreement with an appallingly barbaric regime armed with only his trademark umbrella. The quote has entered the history books for all the wrong reasons. Yet it tells us a great deal about pre-war political discourse. Addressing that society, Chamberlain could assume a certain cultural fluency and an ear for the literary tradition in a way today's speech writers cannot. Had his mission not eventually met with such failure, this reference from the Bard would have passed by unnoticed and been saved from the ridicule to which it is exposed today.

One might ask whether Chamberlain was simply exemplifying the style of speech of his day or if something more significant was going on. In the face of a phenomenon taking hold of the European mainland, which had never been encountered before and for which there was no historical precedent, Chamberlain gestures towards the poetic medium. He projected a favourable outcome by mining the native tradition. He tentatively nods to poetic discourse, which is a suggestive, exploratory and searching means of communication, as he tries to envisage his way through an unnavigable thicket. Perhaps we can feel some compassion for Chamberlain, that absurd old English gent dwarfed by the ominous Goliath looming before him. For people often make allusions to poetic turns of phrase when faced with unfathomable realities. Poetry is the language of love, of fear and of death – it gives voice both to epiphanies and to catastrophes.

For this reason, poetry flowers in civilizational death and rebirth. This is obvious enough in the emergence of romanticism, when feudalism gave way to industrialization or, in the First World War, poetry about the cataclysmic destruction of nineteenth-century ideals giving birth to the modern era. It applies to Shakespeare himself, of course, standing on the interstices of late medieval and early modern England, in the midst of floundering and novel religious and cultural identities. Shakespeare can in this sense rightly be called a bard, after the bearers of that office among the ancient Britons. The bards codified and explicated their people's circumstances and contexts in mnemonic iterations, providing orientation for understanding contemporary events and gesturing thereby to the emerging future. The bardic office was therefore prophetic. Not in the sense of crystal-ball gazing, but by providing orientation. This is not to say there was not a mystical and mythical dimension to the role. A relationship between poetry and some 'beyond' endures to this day in certain approaches to poetic inspiration. As we read in *A Midsummer Night's Dream*,

The poet's eye, in fine frenzy rolling,
Doth glance from heaven to Earth, from Earth to heaven.
And as imagination bodies forth
The forms of things unknown, the poet's pen
Turns them to shapes and gives to airy nothing
A local habitation and a name.

Faced with that which is not yet seen ('things unknown'), the poet's imagination rises on what Keats called 'the viewless wings of poesy', so his pen can explicate things which would otherwise be mere 'airy nothing'. In doing so, intangible things are 'named'; discovered and given semantic currency. This process always interprets things through a particular cultural context (a 'local habitation'): 'Such shaping fantasies, that apprehend/ More than cool reason ever comprehends.'

Poetry is often assumed to be a spontaneous form of discourse, something intrinsically undisciplined, that just springs forth, on 'viewless wings' fully formed. But Chamberlain was clearly conversant in his tradition, his mind was disciplined in the way a decent schooling in literature once ensured. Moreover, to practise the poetic artform was, until recently, something that required robust training, some of the most restrictive rules on form of expression in the stanzas of a sonnet or iambic pentameters. It was until recently intrinsic to poetry that obedience brings freedom. This freedom to express unknown realities was granted only to words arranged according to the strictest of rules, in particular and highly specific poetic forms.

In the post-war era, political and social discourse in the public square has opted for 'cool reason' over against the 'shaping fantasies' of the poetic imagination. A functional, bureaucratic and managerial mode of speech signals the professionalism of the political class. A new form of discipline over language was taking hold, replacing the time-honoured disciplines of a poetic mindset with a new discipline in global education, making people 'smart' or 'professional'. The discipline of linguistic expression is now about functionalism – how well language will achieve particular ends. The discipline of the poet allows language to reveal new ends to its hearers. One is practical, the other fiduciary. To read a poem one has to have the discipline of mind to take on faith the images portrayed, to let the poem reveal itself to you 'as imagination bodies forth'.

Rhetorical devices in everyday speech have become less and less common and any full-blown recourse to the poet's pen, in the public square at least, is rare. This pen has retired to living in avant-garde bookshops, hidden away like the disgraced Chamberlain. The profundity of the poetic medium is certainly still appreciated, particularly in presidential inauguration speeches, for example. But here poetry is often reduced to fulfilling a function. If you look closely at, say, Miller Williams' poem written for Bill Clinton's 1997 inauguration, it is not a searching nor exploratory attempt to give voice to something new, but explicitly states quite the opposite:

> . . . We mean to be the people we meant to be,
> to keep on going where we meant to go.[1]

Here, poetry is employed to exemplify pre-existing parameters, rather than give birth to new means of orientation. The reasons behind the reduction of poetry to mere function in the public square are many and varied. In the first place, function and efficacy has a certain universal or 'transcultural' provenance that makes it appealing in an increasingly globalized context. There is no room here for 'local habitations', for native traditions and shared histories like those once preserved by the bards. It is also important to note poetry's time-hallowed link with the transcendent or supernatural, which loses traction in increasingly materialist and secular societies. Moreover, genuine ideological conflict, at least since 1989, gave way to an apparently enduring settlement, so that there was not the fertile ground of shifting epochs and worldviews, which often prompts the emergence of the poetic voice. When prosaic terms of reference no longer hold sway, people turn to the visionary and exploratory articulations of the poet to find their way through.

The visions articulated by poetic speech cannot be seen through a narrowly delimited Overton Window. Outside of the public square, even everyday communication has been limited to function, in contrast to allusion and exploration. The eclipse of heavy industry by the service sector involved replacement of functioning objects with words and concrete processes with semantic formulations: 'customer satisfaction', 'top-quality', 'economy-size' and 'longer-lasting'. The result is assembly line speech, identikit locutions, the flat-pack sentence. Merely functional discourse is pre-packaged speech, tightly wrapped in clingfilm, clinically neutralized and artificially compounded. Functional discourse, by definition, cannot break the bounds of the presuppositions it serves, for then it has ceased to function. An organic example of this can be heard by people exchanging pleasantries and making small talk. The literal sense of commenting on the weather or saying 'nice to meet you' is unrelated to the real significance of these exchanges, which hides behind the ill-fitting words it wears. For this speech is a way of displaying shared presuppositions and convictions; it functions to put ourselves and others at ease by quickly carving out a shared semantic space. It seeks to diffuse the unknown, the radical, the different: it bespeaks a terror of our being mutually dumbstruck by that awkward sense that we might be estranged from each other.

The language of the contemporary workplace has entirely surrendered to dominance of the procedural, to the bureaucratic (literally, the 'ruler of the office'). It seems designed specifically to enable those initiated in its logic to display their own dissolution to the dictatorship of the bureau, their unquestioned willingness to smooth out anything particular, any 'local habitation', so no compensating reorientation will be required by the organization they serve. For what is actually signified by managerial speak like 'touching base', 'going forward' and being 'onboard'? Submission to an inexorable telos. In the UK, smooth-talking managerial speech had its own anti-bard in Tony Blair. Blair, by stripping out the ideological basis of his political party, removed an alternative worldview from British politics. The result was a managerialization of the political, politics as a play of efficacy. Administrators without portfolio swarmed the corridors of power, 'tsars' from other sectors who exhibited transferable skills. 'Cool reason' defined the assembly line, pre-packaged speech provided the empty *lingua franca* of a soullessly globalized world.

Speech reduced to function is the linguistic currency of ideological settlement, of an Overton's Window whose frame has receded out of sight because everyone is standing too close to the glass to acknowledge its existence. It is the language of unquestioned presuppositions. Its context is like that of Blair's statement, 'Mine is the first generation able to contemplate the possibility that we may live our entire lives without going to war or sending our children to war.' Leaving aside the irony of this statement and not asking how many mothers of military personnel must seethe at his words, such a supposed *pax* means that the exploratory work of the poet is no longer needed. Where people do not battle against things unknown, there is not that impulse that drove Wilfred Owen to give voice to 'the stuttering rifles' rapid rattle' on the Western Front.

To converse functionally is to converse in monological terms and therefore not to converse at all, because neither party can be brought to a fresh place of understanding. It already has its remit carved out for it, its purpose defined. This speech is contrived, it cannot bear spontaneity or authenticity. Functional speech is eminently transferable. It must be capable of being transplanted, easily, into entirely different contexts, where it can quickly resume its connective purpose, the stated end for which it was designed. It is all form and no content. The brand-new, boxed-up laptop will do its work regardless of whether it is purchased by a writer, architect or graphic designer. It seems in and of itself morally neutral, always separable from the unsavoury activities to which it might be turned. Some flat-pack instruction booklets have now dispensed with language altogether. One cannot deny the fact that they work well and function efficiently. Efficiency is won at the price of millennia of linguistic sophistication being undone. Culture dies with language. Local habitations begin all to look the same when deprived of words. Context is nothing where function is everything.

In recent years, however, a phenomenon has arisen that suggests exploratory language and, therefore, the realm of the poetic might be beginning to emerge once again. The preliminary stage is for language no longer to function as expected. Commentators often lazily point to how the internet has enabled harsh and abrasive speech to re-enter public life. Populist speeches frequently exemplify this same turn. As Elena Block and Ralph Negrine put it, 'Populist leaders use abrasive, belligerent, direct and simple language to connect with disenchanted publics.'[2] But it is remarkable how rarely mainstream commentators take issue with the arguments at stake in each case of populism. The most frequent condemnation is language of dysfunction. So Donald Trump was called the 'mayor of Crazytown'.[3] Sometimes commentators opt for malfunction, highlighting the errors in the way the system is working.[4] Yet beneath the condemnations of dysfunction and malfunction is an untouched conviction: that the pre-existing status quo must have been unbroken and efficient, that the problems are not inherent or intrinsic to the system itself. When something is malfunctioning, one does not adjust to the change, one does not just keep going and try to make it work: you replace the rogue element. A malfunctioning car does not lead someone to question the rectitude of automobile transport.

But poetry flowers in civilizational death and rebirth. Maybe the abrasiveness and bad taste on display in the public square actually signals a grave outlook for the allegedly unbroken status quo. The first stage of an unveiling is to acknowledge the fragility of the veil. An exotic dancer begins her act by letting the outer layers of her costume quiver and flutter. In doing so, the reality of what lies beneath suggestively emerges in the imagination of her audience. Perhaps the fragility of the dominant discourse is being exposed; people are standing back from gazing at the permitted vista and seeing their reflections on the glass before their eyes. Poetic speech will describe the contours of the window-frame itself, envisaging something new from the staggered staccato and shattered sentences of the rabble-rousing speech. Much interesting and inventive writing today, while a far cry indeed from populist rhetoric, wouldn't make much sense without the spectre of populism behind it. Among all the discourse available to us today, the genuinely open and exploratory pieces will be those of a better written quality, those that take a more inventive form, those in which the language itself carries both writer and reader somewhere new.

This calls for a rediscovery of discipline that is not forcing everyone into the functional mode of speech. It is the discipline that takes much longer to acquire, from studying a literary tradition, from living among those to whom the tradition is bequeathed and learning fluently the lilts of their speech. It is a discipline today's world cannot countenance, because of its fiduciary character. Bardic discipline flourishes in worlds where faith is prevalent. Poetry makes little sense without faith. Language is pushed to the limits and takes on new forms when the writer is challenging unquestioned presuppositions. Functional prose rests on buzzwords and assumed convictions, clinically neutralized and artificially compounded constructions, serving only to signal that which is being assumed, not inquire into alternative orientations.

An example of writing that displays the more organic discipline with words is Michel Houellebecq's novel, *Submission*, which occupies a cusp-point between civilizational death and rebirth. Indeed, Houellebecq, in a remarkably self-defeating move, opens the novel with its protagonist, François, discussing literature itself as something dying. He calls it 'the *major art form* of a Western civilization now ending before our eyes' [original italics]. François' approach to literature is decidedly late-nineteenth century, for he is a scholar of the author Joris-Karl Huysmans. François argues that 'only literature can put you in touch with another human spirit, as a whole, with all its weaknesses and grandeurs, its limitations, its pettinesses, its obsessions, its beliefs; with whatever it finds moving, interesting, exciting or repugnant'. In other words, returning to Shakespeare, 'Such shaping fantasies, that apprehend / More than cool reason ever comprehends.' This is very like the account of poetry given by Dilthey, a contemporary of Huysmans. Dilthey held that poetry is uniquely able to allow someone to enter into the subjectivity of its writer, which, like Houellebecq, he calls a 'whole' or *Gestalt*, the 'shape' of a person's imaginings or 'fantasies'.

The death of Western civilization is particularly perceptible in *Submission* when François wanders into the Chapel of Our Lady at the ancient shrine of Rocamadour in the Dordogne. A poetry reading is taking place, of the old French nationalist and Catholic poet, Charles Pierre Péguy, another contemporary of Huysmans.

> Mother, behold your sons who fought so long
> Weigh them not as one weighs a spirit,
> But judge them as you would judge an outcast
> Who steals his way home along forgotten paths.

François enters a 'strange state', in which 'it seemed the Virgin was rising from her pedestal and growing in the air' and all Jesus 'had to do was raise his right hand and the pagans and idolaters would be destroyed and the keys to the world restored to him'. But then he concludes, 'Or maybe I was just hungry.' This moment fits the overarching mood of Houellebecq's dismissal of the Western status quo; a confused but largely uncaring tiredness, a *laissez-faire* nonchalance born of decay. Beforehand, François is so exhilarated by Péguy's invocation of 'a handful of earth / So lost to them and that they loved so much' that he says, 'I felt ready to give up everything', 'not really for my country, but *in general* [original italics]. This is passion which is generalized, universalized, rendered transferable and lacking in content, passion artificially arrogated to something considered vaguely worthwhile but not subject to critique. It therefore promptly dissipates into hunger. The chapter closes with him leaving the chapel after he felt 'shrivelled and puny', so, 'reduced to my damaged, perishable body . . . I sadly descended the stairs that led to the car park.'[5]

Submission was published amid great controversy. The same year, Robert Menasse's *Enraged Citizens, European Peace and Democratic Deficits* was awarded the European Book Prize. It is an essay on the challenges facing the EU, which argues for the end of political nation states in favour of an emboldened 'postnational democracy'. Shakespeare's 'local habitations' and Péguy's 'handful of earth . . . they loved so much' are therefore assailed, page after page. Menasse calls national interests 'beastliness', considers those who speak of cultural identities 'zombies from the nineteenth century', and dismisses the 'interests of the voters in the nation-states' as 'demagogic'. A comment about 'the irrationality of a so-called national identity' is particularly telling. The word 'rational' is one of Menasse's favourites. Without a hint of irony, he speaks of EU leaders as those called to act 'like representatives of supra-national reason' and of those who 'share an enlightened mentality that thinks in transnational categories'. 'National interests' are said to be 'contrary to any objective logic'. When nations are dissolved into the EU, he claims, 'maybe the historical ingenuity of reason will once again prevail'.[6]

Menasse thus sets his sights firmly on those 'shaping fantasies' of European identities, those of supposed 'nineteenth-century zombies' like Huysmans, Péguy or Dilthey. But while their 'shaping fantasies . . . apprehend / More than cool reason ever comprehends', Menasse exalts 'cool reason' above all else, seeming actively to want to diffuse language, to put it back to work, atavistically, in service of its prior function, piling more dead soil upon the earth beneath which the sleeping bards lie in their graves. This endeavour involves his application of 'cool reason' to language often found in writing about the EU. He condemns phrases like 'bureaucratic palaces' for the monochrome edifices of Brussels or the alleged 'dictatorship of civil servants'. He criticizes the phrase 'bureaucratic juggernaut', and the repeated use of the term 'mania' to describe the EU's concern for regulation. Above all, he condemns that fusing of the word 'bureaucrat' with the EU official, into the ubiquitous neologism 'Eurocrat'.

But what Menasse does not realize is that such speech – non-literal, hyperbolic, suggestive, metaphorical – is speech which is not fanatical or ill-considered, but arises from a paradigm of discipline as immersion and familiarity in relation to language. It is not undisciplined, even if it is emotive. The freest and most emotive expressions in language were once those that required the most discipline and obedience. This language refuses to be reduced to function for the dominant presuppositions he defends. Menasse wants to flatten out any kind of difference into what he calls different 'mentalities', that is, in his own words, 'national identities [that] have turned into quirks'.[7] But can the differences between, say, Dante, Goethe and Shakespeare be relegated to the realm of the 'quirky', a service-sector word for reducing uniqueness to the level of function? He condemns each nation's 'contradictory feelings and fantasies' as unable to withstand 'rigorous scrutiny'. He is quite correct, of course, for these 'feelings and fantasies' mirror what Houellebecq calls the human spirit's 'weaknesses and grandeurs, its limitations, its pettinesses, its obsessions, its beliefs'. The particular contours of these things, which cannot be universalized by 'cool reason', are captured only by poetic communication, so it comes as no surprise that Menasse takes issue with the style in which his enemies speak.

Both Houllebecq and Menasse – one *enfant terrible* and the other lauded by a pan-continental critical acclaim – occupy a space between a civilizational death and rebirth. This is shown by the tensions of style and genre at play in each. In *Submission*, prosaic speech stands aside so Péguy's poetry can break through onto the page, albeit abortively and without managing to lead François to 'steal his way home along forgotten paths'. For Menasse, the style and structure of Eurosceptic rhetoric must be assailed. Here we have two different reactions to an architectonic shift in the terms of speech, a change in presuppositions that Menasse wishes were unchangeable. Menasse's 'zombies' are actually 'local habitations' and 'names'; particular peoples, in particular contexts, speaking in particular languages, not in the functionable, but woefully stilted, cadence of the transnational polyglot.

What is happening in both books is the first showings of a rebirth of non-transferable speech, speech that cannot be fitted into any context because it no longer merely serves unseen presuppositions. As Michael Schmidt has pointed out, one may be able to paraphrase the sense of a poem, but the poetic utterance itself can never be paraphrased; it can never be transferred into someone else's terms. It is the stubborn differential, the remainder concept, that will not be flattened out by any homogenous impulse. In his descriptions of the way poetry expresses a person's *Gestalt*, Dilthey argued that this singularity can only be expressed in ways innately personal and culturally situated: it can never be wrenched from its particular, concrete context.

Poetic speech takes hold when language no longer serves as a mere tool or cog that can be slotted neatly into place. Poetic speech is speech that has taken back control and that does not express predetermined parameters as opposed to hacking-out new ones, boldly. It is speech that discloses, rather than veils. Poetic speech requires a discipline of language and culture that means the way people articulate things doesn't just reflect how they see things; it actually enables them to see. If we are to witness an epochal rebirth from the ashes so despairingly described by Houellebecq, the old bardic discipline will need to be reborn. Language is then free to give voice to the airy nothing, to give voice to a freedom not prescribed by those who would restrain and restrict our words.

9

Duty

In *Submission*, Houellebecq's François reaches a state of religious intensity like that of the old saints of Christendom setting about to challenge periods of civilizational decline. With what seems like a commissioning vision from the life of St Francis of Assisi or St Catherine of Siena, François says it seemed as though all Jesus 'had to do was raise his right hand and the pagans and idolaters would be destroyed and the keys to the world restored to him', before the scene dissipates back into nonchalant entropy; 'maybe I was just hungry'.

Houellebecq's writing is characterized by this entropy throughout his novels, the entropy of a civilization that no longer offers any enduring meaning to its people. It imprisons his readers, holding them captive, restrains and subjugates them. But the mastery of his authorship is such we do not even struggle in our chains; it is an uncaring tiredness. Western civilization has so emphasized constant gratification and individual fulfilment that a collapse of cosmic meaning cannot rouse any resistance, only submission. An overbearing mood of indifference hangs over his work.

This entropy leaves the reader in a kind of numbness, but it is not without guile. It has the spite a depressive unleashes when his loved ones demand life from him, when they are exasperated by his lack of exuberance. Asked to break free into a vitality he cannot muster, the depressive pours scorn on those who long above all else to liberate him from himself. Houellebecq's entropic weight leaves his readers indifferently captive, unmoved even by the decline of the West. They are carried downstream into an abyss they cannot even be bothered to try to avoid. To ask us to snap out of this entropy is like expecting a suicidal person to break into sudden shouts of joy. The spell of entropy is utterly imprisoning. Its subjects just float downstream with it. Spellbound, they slip ever further into the void.

How are we to break free? Karl Ove Knausgaard's six-volume work, *My Struggle*, was published around the same time as Houellebecq's novels. The work appears at first sight to be autobiography or memoir, yet each volume reads more like a novel, which is how Knausgaard himself refers to the books. It differs from autobiography insofar as, at the point of writing the early volumes at least, he was not a noteworthy historical or cultural figure. He does not write in a way that suggests he wants to set any records straight, nor give an authoritative testimony about important events. It differs from memoir too, insofar as it is written in mostly crisp, fast-paced prose, much more akin to a stream of consciousness than a set of considered recollections. Knausgaard says he wrote it mostly very quickly, in one draft, with no editing or reworking of the material therein. It could be that, as religion and metaphysics whither on the vine, the immediate vitalism of everyday life holds the promise of liberation from the overbearing weight of Houellebecq's entropy.

Knausgaard focuses on so much prosaic detail about day-to-day minutiae it feels absurd. His is 'a realism so thoroughgoing and full of circumstantial actuality that we may as well call it "punitive realism"'.[1] He will describe cracking eggs while making an omelette in an apartment he shared with his partner twenty years previously, list every single item he bought from a small supermarket one morning during his first term at the Writing Academy in Bergen when he was nineteen and list, point-by-point, the steps involved in changing his fractious daughter's nappy in the midst of a family row. This 'level of quotidian detail' appears 'to be beyond the capacity of anybody's actual memory'.[2] It is considered 'punitive' by those who find it only unnecessary and self-indulgent. But, while it is indeed both of these things, the overall effect is not actually one of tedium. *My Struggle* is compelling. It is as deliciously moreish as any stylized novel. The reader is somehow invigorated by it, to return with gusto to the tasks and struggles of daily life.

Knausgaard admits to making up some details when his memory failed him. The literary playing-with-form of the traditional autobiography or memoir means it is right to consider the book's novels, of a genre that came to be called 'autofiction'. In Knausgaard, this genre lacks editorial stylization; it offers the pure, unfiltered, relaying of consciousness as it happened or as the author thinks it happened. In memoir, those excerpts of diaries and recollected augmentations are always configured and arranged in such a way as to highlight how best to interpret certain events, according to the author. The projected future then reconfigures the past, adjusting how that past is viewed by the reader in the present, so the future interpretations might align with the authorial account, for posterity.

Dilthey wrote that human consciousness, when it comes to memory, is structured and functions in exactly the way an autobiographer works. The autobiographer is in the midst of the life being written about, just as any person can only self-reflect on the life he or she is living. Moreover, our memories are highly selective. This is not just indiscriminate filtering, as such, but a filtering led from somewhere below the level of explicit consciousness: 'Memory is pragmatic, it is sly and artful', says Knausgaard and what is actually remembered 'is never given to you to determine'.[3] Vast amounts of detail are unwittingly shorn away from our memories each night, leaving choice fragments that may eventually endure because we apportion them some significance. Human self-consciousness situates the 'parts' of one's life (relationships, events, places, etc.) in relation to the always emergent 'whole', to the sense one has for the entirety of one's life trajectory, what one's life actually means.

Dilthey is of course a modern figure, in the strict sense, whereas Knausgaard would generally be considered postmodern. After reading the 3,770 pages of *My Struggle*, we do not glean a unified essence or sense of the meaning of his life; just a vast, rambling and seemingly disconnected and indeterminate mass of experiences. The indeterminacy applies only to the overarching narrative, however. Every moment in the book feels steadily anchored in narrative as it happens, one doesn't feel bewildered or confused while reading each page. Yet one cannot explain the narrative trajectory of volumes 1–6 in a coherent, meaningful way, let alone in any cumulative or developmental fashion, with concrete outcomes and conclusions. As Jameson notes, the details of *My Struggle* 'have not been transformed or lent some higher meaning; they remain what they were before, transient and of no particular interest'. They are not 'lifted into the timeless eternity of classical literature, posterity and the canon: you can dip into them wherever you like and they will not be any more quotable or Virgilian; they will, in fact, remain quite as nondescript as before'.[4]

A lack of a cohesive sense makes perfect sense for contemporary notions of selfhood. Knausgaard reflects on things like existentialism in the books, but never reaches an account of the self that has enduring veracity. He said in an interview, 'You can never reach an authentic "I", an authentic self.' On writing the work, he says: 'I started to look at the main character – myself – as a kind of place where emotions, thoughts and images passed through.'[5] This was exactly the sort of approach to subjectivity that Dilthey wanted to counter, citing the adversarial position as the Humean 'bundle theory' of the self. For David Hume, the self is a mere 'bundle of perceptions', lacking continuity, direction, significance and stability. Hume's opponents, like Dilthey, feared this would end in something like the uncaring nihilism of twenty-first-century selfhood. Without a consistent sense of self-identity, there could be no developmental trajectory. This disorientation would dissolve into meaninglessness, with its attendant ethical aporias. Hume is upstream from Houellebecq, where we see the effect of the 'bundle self' in all its unmoved morbidity.

While Knausgaard sees himself as a bundle of perceptions. Frederic Jameson, an early theorist of postmodernism, argues that Knausgaard does not present a postmodern self, however. Knausgaard treats all data – thoughts, feelings, shopping lists, arguments, weather, emotions – to the same level of quotidian, prosaic detail, something Jameson calls 'itemization'. This means there is no death of the author, nor any real sense of permeability between himself and social structures, language, nature or the other. That is, Knausgaard does not take the 'bundle theory' to its ultimate end, where even the self dissolves into its surroundings.

While Houellebecq's entropy holds everything captively spellbound and tired by the deadening weight of its downstream current, Knausgaard's vitality assails us like a juggernaut, the din of which subsumes everything into its own narrative voice. The primacy of the authorial voice, says Jameson, means that 'innumerable sentences in these thousands of pages – varied as they may be – fail to pass the supreme test of any postmodern aesthetics, which is the achievement of heterogeneity'. The monological narrative means this is not a 'post-subject' or 'post-human' work, it differs from postmodern notions of selfhood in that it does not arrive at the hyper-Humeanism where even human perceptions are just bundles of external factors, where everything is rooted in other realities and the self is an empty illusion.[6]

Put differently, Knausgaard is stubbornly modern. He will not surrender or submit to the vacuous end, he will not be carried downstream into the empty climax. His relentlessly quotidian detail offers resistance to entropic decay. Against the collapse of the 'big picture' of civilizational history, religion and metaphysics, the human subject still fights battles of seemingly cosmic proportions in the unavoidable duties of everyday life; shopping, cooking, changing nappies, wanting to stay in love, caring for elders, tidying the kitchen, thinking about death, vacuuming the bedroom. The everyday is still vital, still passionate, still full of things so worthy of being fought for that one launches into battle to defend them without even knowing one is going unto war. This is life just being lived. This is the life the depressive can no longer even imagine.

Modern and postmodern notions of selfhood take shape in dialogue with cosmology. Understanding human selfhood requires, by definition, some understanding of our place in the cosmos. The premodern self is called by Charles Taylor a 'porous self', a self permeated with unseen and mysterious realities. In the premodern cosmological scheme of Dante Alighieri's *Divine Comedy*, there is the inferno below earth where sinful people go for their eternal torment, below the earth where we live day-by-day, which is the bottom rung of a ladder of seven heavens, with God situated – *literally* situated – at the very peak. Heaven was, for the premoderns, genuinely in the sky, above the clouds and the starry spheres. There, Jesus Christ was enthroned, his risen and ascended body seated at the right hand of the Father. What today are assumed to be abstract truths derived from some dimension other than this one, like divine properties or characteristics, were once much simpler and more vital realities.

These realities impinged directly and tangibly on everyday life. God was omniscient because of his heavenly vantage point over all the world. God was omnipresent because he sat at the summit of all creation from whence it subsisted, second-by-second, according to His gracious will. Hell was Godforsaken because under the earth you were hidden from God's sight.

The self thus existed in a world where all the forces of nature were thought to be orchestrated, moment-by-moment, by the overarching will of the Most High; that is, He who is situated at the highest point of all. All the events of one's life, the structures of society and the natural world on which people depended utterly, were powered by angels and archangels from their designated positions within the great cosmological scheme. With the maker of Heaven and Earth looking upon all, all that one does was very literally, very concretely, answerable and accountable to Him. This is not to say that pre-modern people were somehow ethically superior to others, that the premodern world was not full of sin and evil and wrongdoing; just that there was an immediate vitality to matters today deemed 'religious' or 'moral', a cosmological scheme whereby human life was integrated and inextricable from the architectonic pattern of an interweaved human and divine reality.

Of course this changed most fundamentally between Copernicus' *De revolutionibus* (1543) and Isaac Newton's *Philosophia naturalis principia mathematica* (1687). The premodern cosmology had Earth at the centre of the cosmos, with all cosmic weight bearing down upon human deeds. Human life was the interface between heaven and hell. As the heliocentric cosmos took hold, the new cosmology that emerged with Newton was mechanistic. The vital, momentary divine force was no longer immediately present or necessary. The allegory of the watchmaker was the best people could hope for. Questions of God were then about the 'origins' of the universe in the distant past, not the miracle of life in which we find ourselves in every moment. Enlightenment Deism may have been a creed relatively few would explicitly espouse, but its basic tenets were influential far beyond its circle of adherents. The authority of the natural sciences draws its contemporaries into its spell, regardless of what they espouse.

When telescopes show that Heaven is not 'up there', the place where God resides lapses surreptitiously into being understood as some dimension other to this one, outside of time and space, in some other place we cannot go in this life, which no high-powered telescope can ever disprove.[7]

The self that emerges from this is called by Taylor a 'buffered self'. Once the cosmos is no longer integrated into mythic, religious or metaphysical realities, those realities were relocated by philosophers and theologians as rooted primarily in human consciousness. The threat of meaningless was too great. The deadening weight of the seemingly inert mechanistic cosmos too horrible to accept. The outcomes for human morality were too dreadful even to contemplate. The modern self is thus 'buffered' not only from what were once seen as mystical forces of nature, but also from the dread fact of cosmic nihilism. This latter buffering is held in place by bulwarks like autonomous reason or conscience. The paradigmatic statement of Enlightenment philosophy, therefore, is Kant's statement that 'Two things fill the mind with ever new and increasing admiration and awe, the more often and steadily we reflect upon them: the starry heavens above me and the moral law within me.' There are now two centres of gravity, as it were; one cosmological, disclosed by natural science, one human, disclosed by human science, the humanities.

Postmodernism similarly emerged against the background of changing cosmology; in this case, the new cosmologies of the twentieth century. At the centre of this was Einstein. The overall effects of relativity and quantum unpredictability feed directly into notions of the self as always relative to culture or language or power structures, always without an absolute anchor like that of Kant's 'moral law'. The counter-intuitive nature of this cosmology feeds into the sense that selfhood is illusory, a protective impulse concocted to shield us against the random volatility of cosmic meaninglessness. The mechanistic cosmos was threatening to humanity for its separability from a sentient cause. But the new cosmos is even worse insofar as it is not only separable, but seems to defy our intuitive norms of stability. Everything charges towards the certain abyss of our sun's supernova. Houellebecq gives human voice to this. A last vestige of human uniqueness still endures in him, but it is just an impotent refusal to care.

Theologians long since had the task of trying to hold together the immovable faith convictions of premodernity – from whence comes Scripture and the doctrines of Christianity – with changing cosmological schemes. On Sunday mornings the faithful still recite the Creed, saying of Jesus Christ that 'He was ascended into heaven and is seated on the right hand of the Father.' Theologians tell us this is framed in the idiom of a naive pictorial language we must demythologize, that Jesus was carried into another dimension outside of space and time. His being seated at the right hand of the father is mere figurative language to denote his divine authority. The weight of what such faith assertions actually mean then bears down upon the mind of the one repeating it in church. An individual's intellectual assent, their reason, is then primary over faith. If God has no right hand because he does not exist in space, the intellect enables someone (or rather, often doesn't) to connect this image to an enduring sense of God's will mysteriously working – *Deus ex machina* – within and beyond the facts of life as explained by natural science.

But, just as with Deism, whichever cosmology is dominant always configures human self-understanding, regardless of whether people subscribe to it consciously. There are no concepts 'more foundational' than 'cosmological ones' and so 'the nature of cosmology is that it is virtually unlimited in its potential influence on human thought, self-understanding and conceptualization'.[8] The philosopher Merlau-Ponty spoke of our way of seeing the world in which we live as a distinctively 'cosmic seeing'. Cosmology is 'the framing reality of the empirical world', our 'pre-conceptual sense of being in the world'.[9] How cosmology functions mirrors exactly what Knausgaard says in a passing remark about a '*Zeitgeist*': it 'comes from the outside, but works on the inside' and '[i]t affects everyone'.[10]

One conceptual tool used by theologians to navigate this territory, is the differentiation between what are called 'first-order' and 'second-order' modes of discourse. The first order includes straightforward, uncritical assertions of the faith. These are those found in

Scripture and dogma, like 'He ascended into heaven.' The second order includes those conceptual constructions that can explain or give critical credence to first-order assertions. Here we make recourse to ideas like God existing in a different dimension to this one, and use understandings of the mythic imagination to point to some demythologized reality. The second order purports to allow people to say 'He ascended into heaven', while never doubting that the throne of the Most High was never seen with an early modern telescope. The second order shows people how they might believe wholeheartedly in the necessary components of the faith, while maintaining intellectual integrity and submitting to the conclusions of modern science.

But what those adopting such terms often fail to appreciate is that the foundational, framing set of presuppositions provided by cosmology – Merlau-Ponty's 'cosmic seeing' – still function within the first-order assertions. The realm of cosmology can be termed the 'zero order'. It is so foundational that it does not even need to be articulated, it doesn't need to be brought to the level of explicit articulation, but surreptitiously conditions everything else. It configures and orientates everything from some subsurface level. The first-order assertions have as their foundation the premodern cosmology. But the second-order assertions are also based in their respective cosmology, which is modern or postmodern. A second-order assertion – like saying 'He ascended into heaven' means 'he returned to a dimension other than this one' – seeks to replace one set of zero-order structures with another. It tries to graft premodern assertions onto the zero order of a more contemporary cosmology. The overall effect, however, is an ongoing schizophrenic conflict in the subsurface consciousness of religious believers.

The first order exerts a gravitational pull back to the old premodern cosmology of the *Divine Comedy*. The second order similarly exerts a pull towards the new cosmology, which threatens to render certain truths of the faith malleable, sometimes even disposable. The second-order assertions will always push towards some newer, more intellectually respectable version of Christianity, which worships the abstract, transcendent 'beyond' of contemporary science. Intra-Christian tensions are today assumed to be products of the culture wars, superimpositions of terms like 'conservative' and 'liberal' onto warring camps within churches. But in truth these impulses are rooted in the zero order, in cosmology. These terms can often be reduced to the degree to which people want either to conserve or play fast and loose with the underlying cosmologies at play. Liberal Christianity tends therefore to lump all manner of Christian teachings in with the outdated cosmology: 'if early Christians were naive in cosmology, they probably got things wrong in sexual ethics too'. Conservatives hold fast even to teachings about hell, of which the contemporary mind simply cannot make much sense.

Contemporary belief therefore suffers from a zero-order dissonance. This dissonance takes shape and affects the way people conduct their lives in faith. This follows from how concepts like divine omniscience and omnipresence are understood, foundationally. That is, they are on the one hand abstract properties, which by faith-informed logic must surely be understood as applying to God. On the other hand, they might be closer to the concrete, vitally present realities they were when embedded in the premodern cosmological scheme. For those in whom a newer zero-order dominates, religiosity or morality belong in a certain category, they can be pigeonholed and filed away under those headings. For one in whom the premodern zero order still dominates, somehow, every moment of life can still be shot through by an all-knowing God who is literally present. This is not some abstract, transcendent, notional way to which to give an intellectual assent, but a vital reality – actually *here* – sharing every moment of our lives with us.

Peculiar as it may seem, this difference is analogous to that between the self that emerges from reading either Houellebecq or Knausgaard. For the latter, the 'big picture' collapse of civilizational history, religion and metaphysics continues apace in the background, but the human being of everyday consciousness still fights battles of seemingly cosmic, all-encompassing proportion in the unavoidable duties of his life; shopping, changing nappies, trying to stay in love, caring for elders, and so on. In Knausgaard, the everyday is still vital, still passionate, still full of things worthy of being fought for ceaselessly. In Houellebecq, the way back to the first order via the second order has been subsumed by the latter. The need to play fast and loose with basic tenets of Christendom has won. The ensuing liberality has unleashed a current that carries his readers spellbound into the abyss.

A human preoccupation with the everyday, not as something separable from matters deemed 'moral' or 'religious', is something extremely hard for people to find their way back to now. The contemporary preoccupation with highlighting differences between how one lives one's life and how one presents one's life is one example of this. Integrity, as a wholeness pertaining across both the public and the private, is a very modern concept. It became necessary to define it because this is a world in which most people now assume they are not sharing their lives with an accompanying intelligence alongside them. Now omniscience has become at best something abstract and ethereal, something easily forgotten or put out of one's mind, but more commonly it is just discounted by agnosticism or atheism.

We have seen that culture mediates between nature and humanity. Culture is porous with the natural world and cultures are thus continuous with natural conditions, not radically separable from them. On an individual and existential level, particular instantiations of human nature are formed on the basis of cosmological understandings. A world without meaning will lead to a self constructed in a meaningless way. A world shot through with divine light will lead to a self that is radiant with that light. This formation of the self takes shape through repeated habits, habits of duty.

In time, ongoing practices become 'second nature', as natural even as breathing or sleeping. Herein lies the wisdom behind monastic rules of life and the importance of regular practices of prayer for believers. Herein one can also understand moments of what the Catholic tradition calls 'heroic sanctity'. For a person for whom living in the presence of God is second nature after years of trying to do decently in every little thing, a moment calling for radical self-sacrifice will be undertaken as 'second nature'. This is understood as the most profound freedom, a freedom that comes only from obedience. Sohrab

Ahmari describes this in the case of the martyrdom of St Maximilian Kolbe, as 'a strange but perfect form of freedom'.[11]

In more pedestrian settings, however, duties performed aright become like the fixtures and fittings in which we live and move and have our being. They progress inward, becoming internalized and embedded within us. They are no longer the work of some herculean effort, with endless self-bargaining against the impulse of gratification or individual fulfilment. They becoming fulfilling in and of themselves and then cease even to be noticed. Duties turn the seemingly inert and meaningless world of modern science into a sublime reality. The world is transformed in and through human duty. Here the heavens and the moral law meet.

Everyone displays this duty to some extent. Its beauty is such that people do not even notice it. A mother rising in the early hours to suckle her infant does not reflect on the merits thereof, nor does the spouse of someone with dementia need to decide whether to help them eat their dinner. These things can be performed as naturally as drinking a glass of water. It can be seen in, say, the way anyone – instinctively – will always place a sheet or blanket over the face of a dead body. Why do we do this? Because somewhere, at some subsurface level, people know that a corpse should not be treated like dead, inert matter. People sense that human life is profoundly, spiritually significant. That which carried life through the world and gave it expression – the body, the eyes and mouth – must be veiled like the inner sanctum of a temple; it must not be treated as a mere bundle of molecules. Yet, in placing a sheet or blanket over a dead person, we would not ask ourselves if we should or weigh the benefits of doing it. It is automatic. It is an act of duty.

Knausgaard certainly does not offer us a way back to Christendom. He is upfront about his inability to believe. But this is not the concern here, what matters is the zero-order functioning below *My Struggle*. By bringing all of daily reality into literature, Knausgaard challenges the separation of the 'literary' (and by default, the 'cultural', the 'humanistic') from the 'everyday'. In the old premodern scheme, everything was embedded in an overarching divine reality. In *My Struggle*, everything is brought into the view of the reader. All that 'punitive' detail, filtered by our 'sly and artful' memories, is present and known. The fixtures and fittings of life, the unremarkable world that dominates day-to-day existence, are brought into literature. The effect of this is to send the reader back into his or her humdrum existence revivified; everyday lives are rendered more literary.

Given this discussion, it is salient that Knausgaard points out in the opening pages of volume 1 of *My Struggle* that '[f]or the heart, life is simple: it beats as long as it can'. The book begins with an extended meditation on death or, rather, on the microscopic processes of degradation and decomposition that ensue immediately after death. 'The moment life departs from the body, it belongs to death', we read, so the body becomes 'one with lamps, suitcases, carpets, door handles, windows' and '[f]ields, marshes, streams, mountains, clouds, the sky'. Yet, while we are surrounded by objects and phenomena from the realm of death there 'are few things that arouse in us a greater distaste than to see a human being caught up in it'. This is the distaste that attends seeing the human body reduced to the level of a mere object, of inert matter – even when, strictly speaking, this is what it is in the case of a cadaver. Yet Knausgaard says this distaste is not 'the result of some form of conscious deliberation' for 'the way we remove bodies has never been the subject of debate, it has always been something we have done, out of a necessity for which no one can state a reason but everyone feels'. He goes on, 'if your father dies one windswept Sunday in autumn', you 'carry him indoors if you can and, if you can't, you at least cover him with a blanket'. What else could be functioning here other than the enduring moral law that tells us human life is infinitely precious, of a different order to other forms of life?

Similarly, it is noteworthy that mausoleums in hospitals are nearly always situated underground. He says we instinctively lower dead bodies 'as fast as possible': a 'hospital that transports its bodies upwards, that sites its cold chambers on the upper floors, is practically inconceivable'. He says 'one might be tempted to believe' this is 'based on some ancient convention that originally had a practical purpose', claiming we possess 'some kind of chthonic instinct' – because 'transporting bodies upwards in buildings seems *contrary to the laws of nature*' (original italics).[12] The vertical axis of the old cosmology holds sway here, the ancient conventions which once had a more practical application, returning bodies to the earth as the soul departed for heaven. Knausgaard thus gives voice, unwittingly, to the enduring power of the old cosmology – that takes shape in ways we do not even notice, through the way we conduct our duty, in this case, our duty towards the dead.

There can be no suggestion that Knausgaard has written some surreptitiously apologetic text, any more than Houellebecq. He explicitly articulates a sort of post-Christian life, of living in a time when 'the great, the divine, the solemn, the holy, the beautiful and the true were no longer valid entities but quite the contrary, dubious or even laughable'. He says 'religion does not know a beyond, not any more'. For the 'limits of that which cannot speak to us – the unfathomable – no longer exist' and 'we have turned everything into ourselves'. Here he revisits the theme of death. We hide dead bodies, he claims, because 'death is the last great beyond'.[13]

At the same time, however, what Jameson saw as a stubbornly anti-postmodern sentiment in Knausgaard's lack of heterogeneity applies also to some extent in his refusal to surrender to the void of meaninglessness that he admits to feeling: '[e]veryday life, with its duties and routines, was something I endured, not a thing I enjoyed, nor something that was meaningful or made me happy'. Yet, in volume two, particularly, he returns in his internal ramblings again and again to the seventeenth century, to the early modern period that is so important in terms of cosmology and metaphysics. Having read Spengler's *Decline of the West*, he came to see 'the seventeenth century as a kind of centre', the point where 'the whole magical, irrational, dogmatic and authoritarian tradition' was separated off as 'old and useless'. It is interesting in this connection that he becomes transfixed, around the same time, with the Book of Ezekiel. This is one of the strangest books of the Bible, with numerous passages that quite simply defy reasonable interpretation. He is transfixed by 'the insane prophet with the doomsday images', the 'sudden shifts between the interior of the visions where angels are buried and humans slaughtered'.[14]

The unfiltered monologue also means that views are expressed that today's standards would consider politically incorrect. He says the welfare state has 'subverted' old values like 'masculinity, honour, violence and pain'. Becoming a father, he observes the typical dads of Sweden where he is living: 'women may have despised these men with thin arms, large waistlines, shaven heads and black designer glasses, who were just as happy discussing the pros and cons of Babybjörn carriers and baby slings as whether it was better to cook one's own baby food or buy ready-made ecological purees'. Observing the crowds around Sweden's museum quarter in Stockholm, he says the period of 'middle-class respectability, national romanticism, health fanaticism and decadence', which gave birth to those institutions, has gone. In place of national romanticism the new idea 'was not human unique-ness but equality and not cultural uniqueness but multicultural society'. The old authoritarian, dogmatic and magical world holds sway again, perhaps, when he decries the feeling of travelling through Norway and everything now looking the same: '[t]he same roads and the same houses, the same petrol stations, the same shops'. Up until the 1960s, he says, 'you could see how local culture changed' as you drove through Norway, but now Europe 'was merging more and more into one large, homogenous country'.[15]

Christianity is at best tangential to *My Struggle* and Catholicism, specifically, almost entirely absent, as indeed it was from Norway until recent immigration. Yet, the old authoritarian, dogmatic and magical tradition seems to be working away behind the scenes, when Knausgaard shares his views on what, in today's conservative Catholic discourse, would be termed the 'contraceptive mentality'. He says 'I had nothing but contempt for precise plans to pinpoint the most suitable time' to have a child. If it was difficult, then 'I *had* to live with it', there 'was *no* way out, other than the old well-travelled route: endurance'.[16] This is someone in whom the old call of duty is still heard and he is as perplexed by his own dogmatic irrationalism as anyone else.

This volume of *My Struggle* also features some of the most lengthy discussions of Christianity. He decides to have his daughter baptized and feels resentful at the pastor's suggestion he should be married to his partner. He touches briefly on Jesus being God's Son and quickly dismisses it as 'a wild notion I could never entertain as a belief'. The Knausgaard who prefers the past is still present, however, when he observes his cousin Jon Olav kneeling at the altar with his family to receive communion during the service. Knausgaard will not surrender to the fragmented, post-human world. Jan Olav seemed 'a whole person, a good person' and seeing him 'drew me up the aisle as well and down on my knees'. Knausgaard says: 'I wanted so much to be whole. I so much wanted to be good.' He thus receives communion, despite being unbaptized, unchristian and entirely unsure of any of the points of faith. When his friend Geir comments on this event, he highlights Knausgaard's singular determination, his 'inability to live a double life', the fact that 'there's a one-to-one relationship between life and morality' in him. Geir concludes that 'you're the only person I know who can take communion despite not believing in God and not commit blasphemy'.[17]

Knausgaard's quotidian reality is the place where freedom from the entropy of meaninglessness can be found. Daily duties prefaced on old cosmology can live on within us and cultivating their residual presence will resist subsumption by the dead weight of cosmic nihilism. We do not live as the saints of old, we do not see Jesus raising 'his right hand' to destroy 'the pagans and idolaters'. But we need not retire to nonchalant indifference either. Each moment of life can still be anchored in meaning, even when a cosmic narrative is not ours for the having.

Knausgaard says 'indifference is one of the seven deadly sins, actually the greatest of them all, because it is the only one that is against life'.[18] Duty battles indifference, it places a sheet over the blank, dead stare of postmodernity. It offers a life we do not need to translate into a projection of timeless eternity. Duty inhibits the construction of a stylized story of our lives, the editing of ourselves around a conceited narrative. A life lived dutifully is a life shot through with the glory of God. Our estrangement from the cosmos might well mean the most we can hope for now is to commune with God in our disbelief. If we can do this without committing blasphemy, however, the keys to the world can be restored to their rightful place.

10

Authority

A few years ago, a group of nomads parked up their trailers and encamped on a patch of disused industrial land on the edge of the Docklands financial district in east London. Urban settings often bring different sorts of people into close proximity, but this was particularly intense. Leaving a glass-walled Manhattan-style skyscraper or entering the lobby to an apartment block near the central precinct, the financial executives got wafts of woodfire smoke drifting over the water of the old docks, bringing with it the sense of some other world existing nearby.

The disjuncture was most intense for those who encountered the nomads' kids. Docklands is immaculately ordered: reflective chrome finishes, symmetrical paving on the ground, neatly spaced bollards around the deep old docks, with share prices and currency values floating in perfect straight lines across the towering shiny buildings. Into this scene entered scruffy, delinquent children looking for trouble. They played among the bustle of the faux-Wall-Street hubris, looking for fun and petty crime. When challenged, these kids were as dangerous as the untamed Pitbull terriers and Alsatians they always had with them. In a couple of seconds a suited passer-by could be set upon, stripped of his briefcase and left languishing and bruised on the concrete.

In areas of London more used to these encampments, these children are known as site kids. These are kids who are born and raised on the temporary habitations called traveller sites in British law. Some of these sites are semi-permanent like US trailer parks, usually homing traditional gypsies. On other sites, the occupants take over unused land without permission. The nomads at Docklands were not of gypsy stock, but were descended from a wave of travelling drop-outs who took to living on the road in the early 1980s. The dream back then was of a life lived without answering to any authority. They moved into old buses and trucks and drove out to the countryside to be close to nature, turning their backs on the rulemakers of Western civilization ('Babylon'). To distinguish them from the ethnic gypsies who have trekked the byways of England for centuries, the press called them 'New Age Travellers'. They invariably claimed for their own a hodgepodge of New Age ideas, like supposedly Native American traditions, Celtic paganism, Eastern mysticism and a dash of Rastafarianism. The highlight of the year for these denizens of the Age of Aquarius was a vast festival at Stonehenge for the summer solstice. By 1984, the numbers encamped around the ancient stones each year had reached 30,000, to the distress of local residents, the press and law enforcement.

Predictably, drugs ravaged these travelling communities. The police – newly empowered and lavishly funded under Thatcher – proceeded to make life difficult for them. After an exclusion zone was erected around Stonehenge in 1985, a notorious showdown occurred in which police in riot gear smashed their way through the windshields of the traveller's vehicles, dragging the inhabitants out over the shards of glass and marching them off, bloodstained, to be arrested. The audacity of trying to live without authority provoked bloody vengeance from the state. Many of the original middle-class visionaries gave up on the dream and left the convoy to return to normality, while some had gone too far to turn back. In a few years, hangers-on had attached themselves to the convoy and overtaken the original new agers in number. Now all manner of oddballs lived on the sites. They were people rejected by mainstream living or with criminal records that rendered them unemployable, or just straight-up addicts who found the travelling lifestyle preferable to sleeping on the streets. These people were hard-edged and spiky. When they descended on an area, most observers would stay well away. People who refuse to countenance any authority at all are not easy to deal with.

The remnants of the early 1980s convoy were tough characters, but their kids were on a different level. When looking at grainy footage of police grappling with the wild-eyed, acid-crazed inhabitants of the old rural sites, we see some travellers holding babies, others trying to usher a toddler to safety. By the time of the Docklands encampment, the second generation had become the site kids. Their upbringing had been brutal. With parents living by the needle and the crackpipe, they'd had to fend for themselves. Some were raised with occasional doses of acid or hashcakes, which permanently altered their developing brains. The New Age roots of the movement had more or less disappeared within a generation. They blared out NWA from their trailers and lived on McDonalds, not vegan stew. They were unschooled and completely illiterate. They all shared a virulent and all-encompassing hatred of the police, whose roadblocks, truncheons and arrests haunted their earliest memories.

The site kids were genuinely lawless. The parents had lived under the mantra 'always question authority', but for their children authority wasn't even questioned because they never really encountered it. Any directive impulse they came up against was coercive. There was an unquestioned assumption that state authority was illegitimate, but even within the inner circle of travellers themselves, violence had replaced law on the sites. The nomads could get by a lot of the time on bartering and *quid pro quo* cooperation, but without authority to keep these functioning, disagreements were dealt with by whoever could lash out hardest and fastest. The nearest the kids got to authority was therefore only ever coercion and intimidation. Authority had been replaced by brute force, it could never be seen by those subjected to it as legitimate or consensual. But an authority that is indistinguishable from coercion has ceased to be genuinely authoritative. Sites that ran on this harsh logic seemed to be, not areas in which people were liberated from oppressive social norms, but wastelands in which more brutal norms drained the life from its inhabitants.

It's hard to imagine what it must have been like for the executives who encountered those kids while going about their life in the bustling financial district of Docklands. The abyss of comprehension between these two different tribes was deeper than even the vast Victorian docks beside which they met. It is relatively easy to imagine someone going about their workaday life, encountering the smell of wood fires and body odour, or a group of unruly travellers' dogs knocking over some bins and being transported for a second back to a more primitive mode of existence. But consider what it was like from the other side, for these kids to glimpse the life of the financial executive. Think of the incomprehensible figures on the share-price screens, the smell of expensive aftershave, the gadgets and gizmos, the purpose of which could not be fathomed after they'd been pilfered. Peering through monochrome windows, these neurologically malformed kids could never make sense of the multi-layered spreadsheets on the workers' computer screens, the technologized symbiosis of man and machine in the gyms, or the driverless monorail trains winding their way between the buildings on raised tracks, like decapitated snakes.

The site kids assumed the executives to be epitomes of obedience; willing subjects of the state and global markets, who have fully assented to the status quo and responded dutifully to its commands. But one might ask if genuine obedience really applies to these executives. Acceptance of the state's norms had become so auto-suggestive that it was not full-blooded assent. They had become unthinking cogs in their master's machines, tasks flickering on and off on command like the LED screens on the treadmill or in the elevators. The unreal artificiality of the environment seems to cast no shadow. The end of history narrative and the unquestioned rectitude of the dominant norms meant these executives were just caught up in something and carried along by it. Just as the site kids never knew real authority, the high-achieving executives had never known real obedience. Obedience, to be called such, must involve a measure of assent, a willing subjection of the will. Otherwise it isn't real obedience, but something closer to mechanization. The executives the site kids terrorized didn't know obedience, only unconscious submission.

The two worlds that collided in the few months of that travellers' encampment are therefore more closely related than they appear. Both authority and obedience had receded, replaced by violent coercion on the one hand and unconscious sublimation on the other. The peculiarity of this situation is intensified if one considers the locale of Docklands and its history. The cluster of skyscrapers sits on a part of London called the Isle the Dogs, about five miles east of the much older financial district of the City of London. There, the Bank of

England had for centuries brought young men from English boarding schools, via Oxbridge, to its mahogany-lined offices. Snobbery towards Docklands still endures in the City, with the 1980s riverside constructions seen as coarser and vulgar counterparts to the older neo-classical style of the City, conjuring images of the brash working-class lads who got jobs on the trading floors during Thatcher's deregulation. In the centre of the skyscrapers towers One Canada Square. It seemed to appear from nowhere in the late 1980s, towering over the eastern side of London, with its pyramid crown containing a floodlight which revolved around the night sky, like the watchtower of a new world order.

The Isle of Dogs itself is odd. It is not a literal island, but a large promontory encircled on three sides by a sudden meander in the course of the river. Maybe it looked like an island to passing seafarers making their way along the misty waters while sailing out into the estuary. Or maybe it always just functioned like an island, in that land access was limited due to the sparse highways connecting the mainland. No one knows the origin of the dogs. Of all the various theories, the most plausible are those connected with King Henry VIII keeping his hunting dogs in derelict farm buildings overlooking the river. Sailors would thus hear riotous cacophonies of barking issuing from somewhere beyond the mist and envisaged hordes of canines prowling on the brooding promontory. The island was a rural backwater up until the early nineteenth century. It had barely navigable marshes that were prone to severe flooding, and was home only to a handful of dwellings, the land criss-crossed by little streams cut into the soil to enable patches of land to be rendered suitable for grazing.

In the seventeenth century, British international trade exploded and exotic goods were shipped into London in ever-greater amounts. Around this time, the Isle of Dogs became a synonym for lawlessness. The ships had to queue for days to get to the City and wily thieves could get down to the water's edge after nightfall to steal from the expensive cargos. Once a thief had alighted back onto the island they could not be caught. Only the initiated knew the hidden pathways through the sodden marshland. A ship's crew setting out after them would end up drowning in the mud, their last gasps intertwining with the barks echoing across the river. The thieves were often children, particularly in the theft of spirits, because they wouldn't drink the noxious-smelling rum or gin they siphoned from wooden caskets before jumping back down onto land. The loss of cargo was so severe that eventually huge inland docks were built on the island itself, where ships could moor in walled enclosures for the days it took to process their goods.

Thus began the heyday of the docks – a vast network of walled enclosures where huge amounts of exotic goods were unloaded to feed the mercantilist economy and bolster the imperial coffers. The Isle of Dogs was no longer a synonym for lawlessness, but now hosted a complex collage of different interests orchestrating themselves into a highly functioning and mutually beneficial system. The force of the monarch was not entirely absent, as the need to pay customs duty on incoming goods was central to the docks' construction. But the walled enclosures of the docks were like quasi-autonomous zones, owned by imperial trading companies, which were the world's first joint-stock companies. These bodies managed global territories like only governments do today, in Britain's far-flung colonies. They thus had their own armies and happily policed their little walled outposts in east London. The lawlessness disappeared. Homes were built for the labourers needed for unloading and moving cargo and the 'islander' came into being, as the new natives of this place were called. People no longer needed to navigate their way across the deadly marshland by night to earn their keep.

Notions of governance, of course, changed through the long nineteenth century and in 1909 the docks were nationalized under one central authority. They continued to grow in capacity and the industrial unrest of the first half of the twentieth century gave the islanders a reputation as tough, unruly and riotous. The old lawlessness of the island seemed to have resurfaced from somewhere deep beneath the earth. One could see criminality as an inevitable by-product of the more coercive authority of the state, disorder as a necessary counterpart to unilaterally imposed order. As the light of authority shines too brightly, it casts a shadow that can engulf it. The shadow-side to the docks is built into the landscape of the island, at a place called

Mudchute. Here, the vast quantity of mud produced by dredging out more docks was piled up, creating a pocket of land that remains undeveloped, strangely immune to the civilizing influence that surrounds it. It even feels subtly lawless today – a handful of fields with a grass-topped mound on which farm animals still graze, in the shadow of the glistening corporate skyline. Some say the mound looks like the Neolithic hill-forts and burial structures that surround the untamed and mysterious old plains out towards Stonehenge. Lawlessness is like the mud of Mudchute, in this case a by-product of overweening authority, something cast onto the horizon when authority ceases to be authoritative.

The docks peaked in capacity in the 1960s, after which cargo ships and container freight reached such sizes that newer docks had to be built out in the deeper waters of the Estuary and the old docks fell into disuse and decay. In the 1970s, a local politician and islander was so frustrated with the area's degeneration he wrote to Downing Street to declare the territory an independent republic. Not much came of it, but food supplies and power lines ran dry for a few days. The state made its boldest intervention with the huge regeneration project of the late 1980s – effectively taking control of all the derelict land for the construction of today's Docklands. Now, there is a network of synchronized temples to the global markets homogenized into a smoothly running machine. The intersecting network of old ships' waterways now lie stagnant and unused between the skyscrapers, their murky water lapping the old Victorian brickwork that encloses them.

During the nomad's encampment, few realized that marauding site kids on the Isle of Dogs had a long-standing lineage in that place. What they represent lurks in the marshland soil – lawlessness, the refusal to countenance authority, piled up into an edifice with weird pagan associations. Yet the history of the island also resonates with what the contemporary executives they terrorized signify – sublimated subjection, the loss of genuine obedience in homogeneous, machine-like existence. The delinquents hopping on the hidden pathways across the old marshlands, with their bottles of rum, live on. And there is a sense in which the all-encompassing and unquestioned power served by the latter-day executive resonates with the way the old docks were nationalized and eventually cleared to make way for the skyscrapers. This power lives on too, in the eye-in-the-triangle of One Canada Square. But in the mid-point of these two bleak and soulless extremes lies the rich tapestry of the early nineteenth-century docks: with its odours of wood-soaked rum, earthy pipe tobacco, saffron and rose water. Its fruitful intersection of interests – its self-governance and clear hierarchies – enmeshed into the patchwork of a properly functioning, fecund whole.

The story of the island, therefore, points to a disappearance of both authority and obedience, which has become so dominant in the West that its deeper aspects usually go unnoticed. Today, the execution of authority and the undertaking of obedience have become as toxic and untouchable as the notion of Empire itself. The imperial past is the forbidden fruit of the average historian, the dangerously unnavigable zone where few are brave enough to wander from the permitted paths.

For authority and obedience are today almost completely unsustainable. Parents are told to squat or kneel before their little children, to give a visage of equality in stature, so as not to talk down and give orders. Statements grounded on self-evident authority are now forbidden by parenting manuals ('Because I said so') and replaced with more amenable inducements ('Wouldn't it be nice if . . .'). For those brought up in this way, as we have seen, the word 'obey' had to be taken out of the marriage rite, for it was seen as unacceptable within a loving relationship. In the workplace, all manner of amenable words for those in authority have taken hold – 'leading', 'managing', 'consulting' – and, for the underlings, an ability to follow orders is rebranded in terms of 'appraisals' or 'feedback'. The military is the last place where one can give a command or follow an order, simply because it was given, without being scoffed at.

Politically, the withering of genuine authority and its obedient response has grown apace over the centuries. Hannah Arendt asked in 1956 if anyone would be able to deny 'that the disappearance of practically all traditionally established authorities has been one of the most spectacular characteristics of the modern world'. One result of this disappearance is that people no longer know what the words mean. Arendt points out that authority is 'commonly mistaken for some form of power or violence', when the truth of the matter is 'where force is used, authority itself has failed'. An authority indistinguishable from force has ceased to be authoritative. Similarly, she says obedience is a mode of response in which 'men retain their freedom' – that is, there must be an element of assent, not blind subjection.[1]

Some might argue here that obedience is what legitimate subjects do in liberal democracy, by heeding the law, participating in voting and so on. But the origins of liberalism point to a different form of assent to dutiful obedience. The quintessential expression of this is Rousseau's social contract – a contractual agreement between equal parties, conditional on maintaining mutually beneficial conditions. Rousseau accepts that the social contract reflects a loss, the loss of the more primitive past when human society was simple enough to self-govern. But today Rousseau is so influential that discussions of authority cannot see beyond him. Any discussion of authority is couched only in terms of establishing the grounds of legitimate authority, defining when one must obey because the command is legitimate, meaning the contract is being maintained.

But a genuinely obedient response is different to contractual assent. It is not conditional. It involves going against one's own will: it compels. Plato drew analogies between the impression of encountering something genuinely authoritative with the truths of reason. Something lucidly true compels the mind to assent because it is self-evident, regardless of how one feels inclined about it. There is no need for external means of violence, it simply grounds its authority in itself – 'because it says so'. In this connection, authority and obedience are Apollonian, rooted in notions of truth, light, order and self-evidence. Traditionally, of course, these solar connections meant authority was often patriarchal, the virile solar energy being considered as potently masculine.

Paradoxically, the Rousseauian ideal is intensified in some anarchist traditions. Noam Chomsky says he 'would like to see communicated to people' the idea that 'every form of authority and domination and hierarchy, every authoritarian structure, has to prove it's justified – it has no prior justification'.[2] That is, it must always be questioned and never have its legitimacy presupposed, it must always be provisionally agreed-to as long as it fulfils contractual conditions. But assuming prior justification to authority is exactly what renders it authoritative; it is this that makes it compel. When something is genuinely author-itative, its prior justification is as self-evident as a geometrical truth, like the three sides of the triangle or the radius of a circle being the distance from the centre to the circumference. Something genuinely authoritative doesn't need to be mediated through an interpretive lens to render it legitimate. It is lawful because it says so.

A different intensification of the contract-theory can be located in that later child of the Enlightenment, Karl Marx. Marx certainly made space for authority in his scheme of history, as something that would be necessary for the proletariat to take hold of things and bring communism to full realization. But his dictatorship of the proletariat was only held to be a temporary and provisional stage before it gave way, eventually, to the complete withering away of the need for any authority at all. While Rousseau points to a primitive uncivilized past, Marx was bolder in directing minds to the rediscovery of this primitive order in a fully industrialized future: the utopian endstate, where each would take according to his need and give according to his ability. Both Rousseau and Marx thus share a key characteristic. This is their respective centre of gravity in some other point in time. For Rousseau, authority serves the social contract as a necessary consequence of civ-ilization, to bring us as close as we can get to the peaceful simplicity of the past. For Marx, authority will expire, because we will rediscover our primeval simplicity through our highly developed future.

The Marxian impulse to assume an ideal state in which authority itself can be done away with has led to the situations where anything authoritative is replaced with brute force, just as the new agers of the 1980s produced the dark wastelands on which the site kids dwell. On the other hand, the Rousseauian impulse to hold that authority should not overrule the will leads to a situation in which genuine assent is replaced with auto-suggestion. If obedience needs to be mediated though individual choice, authority develops into the sinis-ter realm of manipulating choices. Rousseau gives way to behavioural science and nudge theory. The identikit responses of those who are nudged into submission are not obedient, they are the disappearance of obedience. The unnavigable wasteland of lawlessness is inverted into the homogenously robotic system. The old Isle of Dogs can be seen as a photographic negative of the latter-day Docklands. Yet, just as the site kids and the financial execs were more closely related than it seemed at first glance, both the Rousseauian and Marxian extremes of political theory are closely related. They are both products of the Enlightenment and they both share a centre of gravity lying in some other place, a Marxist end or *telos* in utopian communism or a Rousseauian beginning or *omphalos* in our uncivilized past.

But, in the middle, again, stands the patchwork collage of the old walled docks. People once boasted that the sun never set on the British Empire, because it reached all corners of the globe. The sailors making their way through the misty waters on their creaking galleons must have disagreed, for their secret artistry was knowing how to make their way across the darkened night by the light of the stars: observing other suns beyond our own when our own has disappeared from view. Resting in the old docks was, for them, a time when they could stop looking beyond this world to remote constellations and would feast on the bounty they brought to shore. The liberal and the communist, the site kid or the executive, are looking always to some sun behind our sun – some unreachable locus where authority was or will not be needed. But genuine authority grounds its own legitimacy in itself, just as the sun rises in the sky each day. The question facing us today is what might be brought to the shore of human civilization if this self-grounded legitimacy to authority is somehow rediscovered.

To pose this question, the ceaseless argumentation about what conditions make authority legitimate will need to stop. Going about the task in this way already renders it impossible, for what is required is a presumption of legitimacy as something self-evident. What is needed is a profound reorientation, an undoing, somehow, of the refractions of Enlightenment currents of thought into a newly orchestrated whole. The means of approach for glimpsing something so unthinkable is synaesthetic: it must bring together things we simply can't imagine being the same, like seeing smells or hearing the sensation of touch.

At either end of the problem lies the self-will run riot of anarchic outcast or the sublimated self-will of the mechanized citizen. The interstice between the two is like that between animal and machine. One seems all freedom, the other all regulation – but where the two meet and fuse, something other comes to pass.

In this sense the answer will be futurist, in the sense of that term used by Italian futurist painters. They highlighted the plasticity and malleability of man and machine – with Gino Severini, for example, distinguishing 'real analogies' from 'apparent analogies' – the latter being moments where two apparently unrelated things are thrown together to reveal some hidden essence behind each. We must rediscover how legitimacy and authority can be synaesthetically indistinguishable again. It will be like suddenly seeing our own sun in the sky after years of blindness or, rather, after centuries of preoccupation with some other sun behind our sun. It will be like sailors coming to moor in a newly fortified dock and forgetting about the distant constellations that promised to guide us through the dark Enlightenment. We need to be rebooted to function properly with our own solar operating system.

This recalibration calls, firstly, for the acceptance of something as self-evident, so that even questioning it is as absurd as suggesting people look upward to notice the sun in the sky. The modern-day professional has not accepted things because the professional brain is wired into mechanized assent. The site kid is the gruesome product of the romantic hopes for some utopian otherworld. The paradoxical maelstrom of the current age is so disruptive, not least because there is a lack of acceptance that genuine authority is necessary. Our living without it is as unsustainable as human civilization without water. As Arendt writes, in a family setting, the 'helplessness of the child' means one must compel their will to yours, and politically, 'the established continuity of an established civilization which can be assured only if those who are newcomers by birth are guided through a pre-established world into which they are born as strangers'.[3] The reason authority and obedience endure in the military is because in the throes of battle there is only room for that which is necessary. Genuine acceptance of this fact means authority will not be seen as a necessary evil but as a necessary good – a life-living force which mandates ordered existence.

Secondly, there needs to be a rediscovery of authority as that around which things cohere, as the sun sits at the centre of our solar system. Richard Sennet defines authority by saying it is 'an attempt to interpret the conditions of power, to give the conditions of control and influence a meaning by defining an image of strength'. As paraphrased by Scott Beauchamp, 'authority is not about coercion', but about 'the very context by which power, control and strength are granted coherence'.[4] Authority binds the whole together and therein lies its integrity. Authority defines what is 'fitting' and therein lies its self-evidence. That which is genuinely authoritative encounters us like the cadence of a rhyming couplet or a truth of geometry. Authority is like that concluding note of Beethoven's Fifth discussed previously, after which the audience would never even think of asking if the piece could have ended in any other way. The arbitrary dies at the hands of the authoritative.

Thirdly, a rediscovery of authority and obedience will obviously be a rediscovery of hierarchy, social and cosmic. The sun was assumed to sit enthroned over the lesser planets of the ancients, which each took their place in a gradated order, just as the sun was itself understood to be under Jupiter and Mars, which were themselves under archangelic powers and ultimately God himself. As Arendt states, the difference between an authoritative regime and a totalitarian or despotic regime is that the latter 'rules in accordance with its own will or interest', while the former has a source which is 'always a force external and superior to it'.[5] The truly authoritative voice speaks from a duty to the 'law' to which it is answerable and which it has not merely constructed. That which is genuinely authoritative derives its authority from the same hierarchy within and by which it commands. Forcing together a religiously and culturally plural society on the shared basis only of being willing contractees threatens to cast a shadow that will engulf it. Authority differentiates. Yes, it builds walls and guards them, because limits and boundaries are necessary and desirable, human communities require them. As Beauchamp writes, 'our culture's pervasive misapprehension and fear of authority derives, in large part, from our loss of community'.[6] Moreover, boundaries mandate freedom, because they preserve the possibility of dissent. Transgression needs lines to cross. Even unruly freedom requires obedience.

To consider authority and legitimacy to be indistinguishable again is an act of synaesthetic recalibration, by which two apparently different things are seen to share a common essence. The encounters between site kids and executives give an indication of how this can happen, insofar as they both share the loss of genuine authority and obedience, respectively. Moreover, each of these losses follows from Rousseauian and Marxian Enlightenment impulses, which hold to a centre of gravity beyond this time, a sun behind our sun. Our task is to knit and weave a presumption of legitimacy back into authority – permitting the genuinely authoritative action and its properly obediential response. The interweaving needs to be so tightly embedded that the questioning of authority becomes the exception and not the norm once again. Indeed, a point where the very questioning of authority is almost forgotten, so indistinguishable is authority from its grounding legitimacy.

Such a moment can be envisaged as like those moments when the executive seems indistinguishable from the site kid. How are we to make sense of this absurd proposition? Undoing the refractions of the Enlightenment to see new singularities does not come easy. But a few years before the Docklands encampment an event occurred on the Isle of Dogs which promises to point us in the right direction. It happened at Mudchute. On the summer solstice in 1992, these fields with their mock Iron Age hillfort had themselves been the site of a traveller festival. The group responsible had been playing cat-and-mouse with the police out in the countryside for months, throwing illegal techno parties and aggravating landowners to the extent they'd been all over the national news that summer. They decided to set up camp near Docklands as a dramatic up-yours to the establishment.

This particular group had a fixation with the number 23. It was painted all over their backdrops and vans, on their t-shirts and hoodies, on the stickers and flyers they used to advertise their events. The reasons for this are to be found in the still perceptible New Age routes of the convoy, although it had since been redressed in cyber clothes and the folk and reggae had given way to driving electronic rhythms. The esoteric and New Age associations of the number 23 are associated particularly with Robert Anton Wilson's 1960s book *Cosmic Trigger*, almost a sacred text for the Age of Aquarius.

But these lawless nomads were locked in battle with the British constabulary, who soon encircled the Mudchute party in their riot gear and droned overhead in their helicopters. The esoteric associations of the travellers might seem a million miles away from the typical policeman, but in Britain there is a long-running and mysterious interrelationship between the police and the freemasons. Just as the romantic, Aquarian lawlessness of the travellers has its roots in the Enlightenment, like the false prophet of authority's final death, Marx, freemasonry too is, contrary to its founding legends, an Enlightenment invention. The mason tries to harness cosmic order under will, mediating all through individual choice, eradicating the obedience of the popular religious devotion of the less well developed. The freemason is fixated with the number 33 – the highest degree of initiation of the masonic lodge.

With these two apparently different groups converging on Mudchute – the night in question seems a very strange night already. But things take a curious turn when we penetrate more deeply into what these numbers 23 and 33 were held to signify by their respective devotees. Because, for all the superficial differences between the two groups, their numerical identities were held to be representative of the same thing. And this is a distant constellation – the sun behind our sun: the so-called Dog Star, Sirius. Why Sirius is called the Dog Star is more mysterious than even the naming of the Isle of Dogs itself. Its history is full of strange occult connections, from the Dogon tribe of sub-Saharan Africa to the alignment of it with the Great Pyramids of Giza during the 'dog days' of August.

But the point is not just that these sworn enemies actually shared a deep affinity, being products of the Enlightenment, squinting to see some sun behind our sun. The point is rather that, by calling to mind this night, we can envisage the moment where they became indistinguishable. For the party in question only lasted a few hours before the police weighed-in. One aspect of the battle that ensued was passed into traveller folklore and spread across the country. It was well known that the police, entering into a situation likely to get nasty, would remove their identifying numbers from their uniforms, so no pictures or video footage would render them liable to litigation for undue violence. But, on this night, the police who set in to the scene placed on their jackets the number 33; deliberately trying to freak the travellers out by being brazen about their freemasonic allegiances. It worked, but only because the revellers, covered in the number 23, didn't realize this wasn't a battle between two opposite extremes – the sworn enemies were on the same side, the side of Sirius, the sun behind the sun.

Let us imagine the scene in the moments before the sound systems were switched off and the arrests began. The police are beating their shields steadily as they encircle the encampment, to intimidate the revellers. But neither side realizes that the steady beat of the truncheons synchronizes perfectly with the 4/4 bass drum of the music. The police dogs too, barking and straining at their leashes at the front police line, seem like mirror images of the travellers' dogs rushing to the scene of the attack to protect their masters. And, as the police set upon the crowd, it seems less like a battle between two warring groups, but more like a perverse dance. A traveller ducks under a policeman's arm, causing him to circle round 360°, another suddenly shifts to one side so a policeman's lunge leads to an abrupt stop and turn in time to the music. Another tries to grab a reveller by the scruff of the neck and accidentally grabs a traveller's hand, so for a few seconds it looks like they're holding hands and pirouetting.

We can now see that two worlds can't collide, because there is only this one world. Attempts to orientate oneself on an imagined elsewhere ricochet back to earth and then bounce off each other as warring cultures. When this point is heeded, seemingly unrelatable things can take shape around each other properly once again. The restrained lives of those who always challenge any authority, as well as those caught up in a manipulated assent, can then be set free. Their obedience will issue immediately, simply because that was what was asked of them. Their freedom is their obedience, their obedience is freedom.

Notes

1 Allegiance

1 Quoted in *Greenham Women Against Cruise Missiles*, Centre for Constitutional Rights Legal Education Pamphlet, New York, p. 2

2 Barbara Harford and Sarah Hopkins (eds), *Greenham Common: Women at the Wire*, London: The Women's Press Limited, 1984, p. 16

3 Ibid., p. 16

4 Lynchcomb, *At Least Cruise is Clean*, Niccolo Press, p. 5 n

5 Harford and Hopkins, *Women at the Wire*, p. 10

6 Ibid., p. 94

7 Dora Russell, 'Foreword', in Lynne Jones (ed.), *Keeping the Peace*, London: The Women's Press Limited, 1984, pp. viii–xi, p. xi

8 Lynne Jones, 'Introduction', in *Keeping the Peace*, pp. 1–7, 4

9 Tamar Swade, 'Babies Against the Bomb: A Statement', in *Keeping the Peace*, pp. 64–8, pp. 64–6

10 Ibid., p. 67

11 Harford and Hopkins, *Women at the Wire*, p. 80

12 Swade, 'Babies Against the Bomb: A Statement', p. 67

13 Harford and Hopkins, *Women at the Wire*, pp. 74–6

14 Raymond Williams, *Culture and Society 1780–1950*, Harmondsworth, Middlesex: Penguin Books, 1963, p. 18

15 Wendell Berry, *What Are People For?*, Berkeley, California: Counterpoint, p. 45

16 Christopher Lasch, *The Culture of Narcissism: American Life in an Age of Diminishing Expectations*, New York, London: W. W. Norton & Company, 2018, p. 92

17 Paul Embery, *Despised: Why the Modern Left Loathes the Working Class*, Cambridge: Polity, 2021, pp. 18 and 58

2 Loyalty

1 Helen Andrews, *Boomers: The Men and Women Who Promised Freedom and Delivered Disaster*, New York: Sentinel, 2021, p. 195

2 Christopher Lasch, *The Revolt of the Elites and the Betrayal of Democracy*, New York: W. W. Norton & Company, 1995, p. 17

3 Jonathan Haidt, *The Righteous Mind: Why Good People Are Divided by Politics and Religion*, New York: Penguin Books, 2012, p.6

4 Ibid., pp. 11 and 12

5 Ibid., p. 53

6 Ibid., p. 216

7 Ibid., pp. 167–8

8 Ibid., p. 313

9 Ibid., p. 316

10 Ibid., pp. 369–70 and 316

11 David Goodhart, *The Road to Somewhere: The New Tribes Shaping British Politics*, London: Penguin Books, 2017, p. 1

12 Ibid., p. 8

13 Ibid., p. 12

14 Ibid., pp. 3 and 13

15 Ibid., p. 115

16 Ibid., p. 42

17 Ibid., p. 81

18 Ibid., p. 114

19 Ibid., pp. 12–13

20 Ibid., pp. 22 and 111

21 Ibid., pp. 6 and 12–13.

22 Ibid., p. xix

23 Ibid., p. 215

24 Ibid., p. 233

25 Ibid., p. 4

26 Ibid., p. 21

27 Ibid., p. 111

28 Berry, *What Are People For?*, p. 85

29 Embery, *Despised*, pp. 18 and 58

30 Lasch, *Narcissism*, p. 45

31 Ibid., p. 103
32 Ibid., quoting Thomas Freeman, pp. 284–5
33 Ibid., p. 287
34 Ibid., p. 286
35 Peter Sloterdijk, *Bubbles Volume I: Microspherology*, Pasadenia, California: Semiotext(e), 2011, p. 12
36 Jean-Pierre Couture, *Sloterdijk: Key Contemporary Thinkers*, Cambridge: Polity, 2016, p. 42
37 Sloterdijk, *Bubbles*, p. 12
38 G. K. Chesterton, *The Defendant*, London: J. M. Dent, 1907, p. 166

3 Deference

1 Charles Dickens, *Oliver Twist*, London: J. M. Dent, 1946, pp. 88–9
2 Ibid., p. 297
3 Ibid., p. 267
4 Gertrude Himmelfarb, *The Spirit of the Age: Victorian Essays*, New Haven, Connecticut: Yale University Press, 2007, p. 106
5 G. K. Chesterton quoted by Ian Ker in *Chesterton: A Biography*, Oxford: Oxford University Press, 2011, p. 164
6 Ker, *Chesterton*, p. 169
7 George Orwell, *The Penguin Essays of George Orwell*, London: Penguin Books, 1994, p. 37
8 Ibid., p. 59
9 Ker, *Chesterton*, p. 165
10 Ibid., p. 55
11 Orwell, *Essays*, p. 55
12 Dickens, *Oliver Twist*, p. 53
13 Ibid., p. 325
14 Goodhart, *The Road to Somewhere*, p. xvi
15 Berry, *What Are People For?*, p. 77
16 Mark Fisher, *Capitalist Realism: Is There No Alternative?*, Hampshire: Zero Books, 2009, p. 19
17 Ibid., p. 21

18 Ibid., p. 21
19 Ibid., p. 21
20 Ibid., pp. 27–8
21 Ibid., pp. 32–3
22 Ibid., p. 37
23 Ibid., p. 28
24 Lasch, *Narcissism*, p. 5
25 Ibid., p. 45
26 Ibid., p. 44
27 Ibid., p. 73
28 Fisher, *Capitalist Realism*, pp. 206 and 210
29 Ibid., p. 68

4 Honour

1 Fritjof Capra, *The Tao of Physics*, London: HarperCollins, 2010, p. 1
2 Andrews, *Boomers*, p. 37
3 Ibid., pp. 106–7
4 Brian Magee, *The Tristan Chord: Wagner and Philosophy*, New York: Metropolitan Books, 2000; Wagner's Diary quoted on p. 135; Magee quote from p. 137
5 Ibid., p. 132
6 Ibid., p. 133
7 Ibid., p. 170
8 C. S. Lewis, *The Four Loves*, London: HarperCollins, 1960, pp. 113 and 133
9 Magee, *Tristan*, p. 167
10 Quoted in Ibid., p. 170 [original emphasis removed]
11 Joseph Sobran, *The National Review Years: Articles from 1974 to 1991*, Vienna, Virginia: FGF Books, 2017

5 Obligation

1 Jacques Derrida, *Archive Fever: A Freudian Impression*, Chicago: Chicago University Press, 1995, pp. 1–2

2 Wilhelm Dilthey, *Selected Works Volume 1: Introduction to the Human Sciences*, Princeton, NJ: Princeton University Press, 1989, pp. 18 and 141

3 Ibid., p. 101

4 Ibid., pp. 49, 79, 490

5 Wilhelm Dilthey, *Selected Works Volume 2: Understanding the Human World*, Princeton, NJ: Princeton University Press, 2010, p. xvii

6 Ibid., p. 24

7 Thomas Chatterton Williams, *Unlearning Race: Self-Portrait in Black and White*, New York: W. W. Norton, 2019

8 Helen Pluckrose and James A. Lindsay, *Cynical Theories: How Activist Scholarship Made Everything About Race, Gender, and Identity*, Durham, North Carolina: Pitchstone Publishing, 2020, p. 19

9 Ibid., p. 30

10 Ibid., p. 193

6 Respect

1 Christopher Caldwell, *The Age of Entitlement; America Since the Sixties*, New York: Simon & Schuster, 2020, p. 99. Caldwell uses the phrase 'habits of respect' as an example of one of the things Ayn Rand opposed in urban environments, something from which people need to be 'freed'.

2 Ben Sixsmith, 'It's Time to Stop Blaming Boomers', *Unherd*, 18 January 2021

3 Caldwell, *Entitlement*, p. 165

4 Pluckrose and Lindsay, *Cynical Theories*, pp. 115 and 123

5 Williams, *Unlearning Race*, p. 21

6 Pluckrose and Lindsay, *Cynical Theories*, p. 124

7 Jean-Paul Sartre quoted by Caldwell, *Entitlement*, p. 121

8 Williams, *Unlearning Race*, p. 63

9 Caldwell, *Entitlement*, p. 17

10 Ibid., p. 161

11 Elizabeth Lasch-Quinn, *Race Experts: How Racial Etiquette,*

Sensitivity Training, and New Age Therapy Hijacked the Civil Rights Revolution, Maryland: Rowman & Littlefield, 2001

12 Williams, *Unlearning Race*, p. 138

13 Ibid., p. 76

7 Responsibility

1 George Monbiot, 'The New Chauvinism', *Guardian*, 9 August 2005

2 George Monbiot, 'Brexiters, Beware: If the Ties that Bind Us Unravel, Tyranny May Soon Follow', *Guardian*, 17 November 2017

3 Ibid.

4 Nathan Lyons, *Signs in the Dust: A Theory of Natural Culture and Cultural Nature*, Oxford: Oxford University Press, 2019, p. 2

5 Ibid., p. 85

6 Peter Wohlleben, *The Hidden Life of Trees: What they Feel, How they Communicate – Discoveries from a Secret World*, Vancouver and Berkeley: Greystone Books, 2016

7 Nikolaus Pevsner, *The Englishness of English Art*, London; Penguin Books, 1956, p. 15

8 Peter Ackroyd, *Albion: The Origins of the English Imagination*, London: Vintage Press, 2004, pp. 61–2

9 Ibid., pp. 36 and 230

10 Ibid., pp. 230–1

11 Robert Winder, *The Last Wolf: Hidden Springs of Englishness*, London: Little, Brown Group, 2017, p. 4

12 Embery, *Despised*, pp. 82–3

13 Ibid., p. 107

14 Berry, *What Are People For?*, pp. 134–5

15 Roger Scruton, *Green Philosophy: How to Think Seriously About Saving the Planet*, London: Atlantic Books, 2013, pp. 9–11

16 Ibid., pp. 9–11

8 Discipline

1 Scruton, *Green Philosophy*, pp. 9–11
2 Elena Block and Ralph Negrine, 'The Populist Communication Style: Towards a Critical Framework', *International Journal of Communication* 11(2017), pp. 178–97, 190
3 Joanna Walters, '"We're in Crazytown": A Week of Dysfunction in the Trump White House', *Guardian*, Friday 7 September 2018
4 Simon Tisdall, 'American Democracy is in Crisis, and not just because of Trump', *Guardian*, Tuesday 7 August 2018
5 Michel Houellebecq, *Submission*, London: Random House, 2016
6 Robert Menasse, *Enraged Citizens, European Peace and Democratic Deficits*, London: Seagull Books, 2016
7 Ibid.

9 Duty

1 Colin Burrow, 'Fiction and the Age of Lies', *London Review of Books*, Vol. 42 No. 4, 20 February 2020
2 Christian Lorentzen, 'Sheila Heti, Ben Lerner, Tao Lin: How "Auto" is "Autofiction"?', *Vulture Magazine*, 11 May 2018
3 Karl Ove Knausgaard, *My Struggle: Volume 3*, London: Vintage, p. 10
4 Fredric Jameson, 'Itemised', *London Review of Books*, Vol. 40 No. 21, 8 November 2018
5 Joshua Rothman, 'Karl Ove Knausgaard Looks Back on "My Struggle"', *New Yorker*, 11 November 2018
6 Jameson, 'Itemised'
7 Amos Funkenstein, *Theology and the Scientific Imagination from the Middle Ages to the Seventeenth Century*, Princeton, NJ: Princeton University Press, 1986, pp. 202–4 and 327ff
8 Oliver Davies, Paul Janz and Clemens Sedmek, *Transformation Theology*, pp. 15 and 25
9 Ibid., pp. 27–9
10 Knausgaard, *My Struggle: Volume 3*, p. 4

11 Sohrab Ahmari, *The Unbroken Thread*, London: HarperCollins, 2021, p. 7
12 Karl Ove Knausgaard, *My Struggle: Volume 1: A Death in the Family*, London: Vintage, 2009, pp. 1–10
13 Ibid., pp. 247–50
14 Ibid., pp. 75, 314, 368
15 Knausgaard, *My Struggle: Volume 2*, pp. 142–3, 100, 439, 76
16 Ibid., p. 242
17 Ibid., pp. 509–10, 531, 534
18 Ibid., p. 663

10 Authority

1 Hannah Arendt, *Between Past and Future*, London: Penguin Classics, 1961, pp. 1–6
2 Noam Chomsky, *On Anarchism*, London: Penguin Books, 2014
3 Arendt, *Between Past and Future*, pp. 1–6
4 Scott Beauchamp, Archived Blog Post, http://www.scottbeauchamp.com/blog
5 Arendt, *Between Past and Future*, pp. 1–6
6 Scott Beauchamp, Archived Blog Post

Index